What Perennial Where

Roy Lancaster

What
Perennial
Where

ROY LANCASTER

DORLING KINDERSLEY
London • New York • Sydney • Moscow

A DORLING KINDERSLEY BOOK

EDITOR Anna Cheifetz
ART EDITOR Helen Robson
MANAGING EDITOR Jonathan Metcalf
MANAGING ART EDITOR Peter Cross
PRODUCTION MANAGER Michelle Thomas
DTP DESIGNERS Mark Bracey, Robert Campbell

First published in Great Britain in 1997 by
Dorling Kindersley Limited, 9 Henrietta Street, London WC2 8PS
Visit us on the World Wide Web at http://www.dk.com

A CIP catalogue record for this book is available from the British Library

ISBN 0–7513–0447–6

Text film output by The Right Type, Great Britain
Reproduced by Colourscan, Singapore
Printed and bound in Great Britain by Butler and Tanner,
Frome and London

CONTENTS

How This Book Works

IN THIS BOOK, my aim is to help you choose the most suitable perennials for a given garden situation or special ornamental effect, taking the characteristics of different plants and your local growing conditions into consideration. The book is divided into five sections: Soil and Aspect, Specific Uses, Floral Effect, Foliage Effect, and Specialist Plants. Within each section, I give a choice of plants suited to your particular needs and lists of additional planting suggestions. All perennials featured are herbaceous (dying back to below ground level in winter) unless described as evergreen or semi-evergreen.

WHAT IS A PERENNIAL?

I have defined perennials in this book as mainly non-woody plants that live for three years or more. Most are herbaceous, losing their leaves and dying down below ground level, usually in autumn or winter. Some are evergreen, retaining their foliage throughout the winter months. A minority of perennials, including bamboos, have woody stems and evergreen leaves. Subshrubby perennials, such as *Lavatera* and *Perovskia*, are a further group that develop a woody or hardened base. This base may survive low winter temperatures even if the rest of the plant is killed off.

KEY TO HARDINESS SYMBOLS

Hardiness is a measure of a plant's ability to withstand winter cold. It can vary depending on available shelter, favourable localized conditions, natural variations in a plant's cold-tolerance, duration of low temperatures, and exposure to frost. Many otherwise hardy plants may be damaged by late spring frosts once new growth has begun. The symbols in the book are a guide to a plant's cold-tolerance and err on the side of caution.

❄❄❄ *Fully hardy – will survive winter outside in temperate climates.*

❄❄ *Semi-hardy – may require winter protection outside in temperate climates.*

❄ *Tender – may require winter protection outside, even in mild areas. Suitable for growing under glass.*

KEY TO pH ACIDITY SYMBOL

The majority of plants will grow in most soils. Those that require lime-free soil are highlighted with this symbol.

PH ▼ *Requires lime-free soil*

BOTANICAL • AND COMMON PLANT NAMES
Below each plant's botanical name is the common name or, if none exists, the generic name.

LIGHT LEVEL, HARDINESS, AND ACIDITY •
Symbols for light level and hardiness are given for all plants; if a plant requires lime-free soil, a pH symbol will appear (see boxes for key to symbols).

Perennials with Strap- or Sword-shaped Leaves

PERENNIALS WITH CLUMPS of long, narrow leaves are irresistible and always striking. Regardless of whether the leaves stand stiff and upright, or bend and arch in a more graceful manner, they are valuable for contrasting with more conventional, broad-leaved perennials in beds or borders, and can also be used as dramatic specimen plants.

Iris pseudacorus 'Variegata'
YELLOW FLAG
☼ ☀ ❄❄❄ ‡↔
A vigorous iris for wet sites, form large patch of tall green leaves w white or creamy yellow bands. T yellow flowers are borne on erec

Arundo donax 'Macrophylla'
ARUNDO
☼ ❄❄❄ ‡5m (15ft) ↔2m (6ft)
This giant, evergreen grass produces long, arching, glaucous leaves, and bamboo-like stems flaunting feathery plumes in summer. It prefers a warm, sheltered site.

EVERGREEN PERENNIALS W STRAP- OR SWORD-SHAPED
Beschorneria yuccoides
Crocosmia paniculata
Dianella tasmanica
Eryngium eburneum, see p.22
Eryngium pandanifolium
Iris confusa
Iris foetidissima
Watsonia pillansii
Yucca filamentosa
Yucca recurvifolia

Eryngium agavifolium
ERYNGIUM
☼ ❄❄ ‡1.2m (4ft) ↔60cm (24in)
The sharply toothed, glossy, evergreen leaves form a striking, erect clump, above which sturdy stems carry cylindrical heads of tiny, greenish white flowers in summer.

FOLIAGE EFFECT

Crocosmia 'Lucifer'
MONTBRETIA
☼ ☀ ❄❄ ‡1.2m (4ft) ↔45cm (18in)
A bright and cheerful perennial, forming a clump of robust, sword-shaped leaves. Its arching, branched spikes of brilliant red, late-summer flowers are good for cutting.

Hemerocallis 'Gentle Shepherd'
DAYLILY
☼ ☀ ❄❄❄ ‡65cm (26in) ↔1.2m (4ft)
During summer, the bold clump of semi-evergreen, narrow, arching green leaves is topped by wide-spreading, ivory-white flowers with green throats.

Iris sibirica 'Perry's Blue'
IRIS
☼ ☀ ❄❄❄ ‡1.2m (4ft)
Erect clumps of narrow, grass-li are joined in early summer by b flowers on upright, soldier-like winter seed capsules are also de

116

KEY TO LIGHT LEVEL SYMBOLS

Light preferences are shown with the following symbols; more than one indicates a range of tolerance.

☼ *Full sun – prefers, or even requires, as much sun as possible.*

☀ *Partial shade – tolerant of (some even prefer) limited or indirect sunlight.*

☀ *Shade – will grow in a site receiving low light, such as under a tree canopy.*

• PLANT DESCRIPTION
Gives features of interest such as flowering time, distinctive traits, and preferred sites or conditions.

PLANT NAMES

Currently accepted botanical species and cultivar names are used throughout this book. Common names in general use are given, and where none exists, the generic name is repeated, or else an English name common to the whole genus or group (such as "pinks") is given. Both botanical and common names are indexed.

PLANT DIMENSIONS

Plant dimensions vary depending on growing conditions. Sizes are a guide to mature size in average conditions. The height includes flower stems, when appropriate.

↕	*Average height*
↔	*Average spread*
↕↔	*Average height and spread*

SOIL AND ASPECT

To help you choose perennials suited to the conditions in your garden, this section suggests small, medium-, and tall-growing plants for a range of different soil types and light conditions: *Heavy clay soil, Sandy/free-draining soil, Lime-free soil, Alkaline soil, Dry soil in sun or shade, Moist soil in sun or shade, Warm sheltered sites.*

SOIL & ASPECT

PERENNIALS WITH STRAP- OR SWORD-SHAPED LEAVES

Sisyrinchium striatum 'Aunt May'
SISYRINCHIUM
☼ ✳✳✳   ↕ 50cm (20in) ↔ 30cm (12in)

This iris-like perennial has striking fans of sword-shaped, grey-green leaves, boldly striped creamy yellow. In summer, it bears straw-yellow flowers in stiff spikes.

'Wrexham Buttercup'
LILY
☼   ↕ 1.2m (4ft) ↔ 60cm (24in)

arching, narrow green leaves ennial form a dense clump. Its heads of rich yellow flowers on strong stems in summer.

Yucca flaccida
YUCCA
☼ ✳✳✳   ↕ 55cm (22in) ↔ 1.5m (5ft)

Reliable and evergreen, this yucca forms a bold rosette of narrow, dark blue-green leaves with wispy marginal fibres. Large heads of ivory flowers emerge in summer. ♔

macrophylla
ARIA
✳✳   ↕↔ 30cm (12in)

ergreen perennial with lance-conspicuously veined leaves, and es of pink to red flowers borne ummer into autumn.

Phormium tenax
NEW ZEALAND FLAX
☼ ✳✳   ↕ 4m (12ft) ↔ 2m (6ft)

Few perennials are as eye-catching as this flax, with its sword-shaped, glaucous-grey, evergreen leaves, and statuesque panicles of waxy, dark red flowers in summer. ♔

HERBACEOUS PERENNIALS WITH STRAP- OR SWORD-SHAPED LEAVES

Agapanthus 'Blue Giant', see p.84
Asphodelus albus
Bletilla striata
Crinum x powellii, see p.40
Crocosmia 'Emily McKenzie'
Gladiolus communis subsp. *byzantinus*, see p.33
Hemerocallis fulva 'Europa'
Iris 'Shelford Giant'
Kniphofia 'Royal Standard'
Moraea spathulata
Nerine bowdenii

117

FOLIAGE EFFECT

● **HEIGHT AND SPREAD**
Gives the average ultimate size of the plant, in metric and imperial.

● **THUMB MARKER**
Identifies each of the five sections in the book (see right).

● **OTHER PLANTS**
Lists more plants suitable for the site or effect, with page references given for those illustrated in other sections.

SPECIFIC USES

This section suggests perennials for specific garden sites: *Hedge bottoms, Rock gardens and screes, Bog gardens and waterside areas;* for specific uses: *Containers, Borders, Ground cover, Naturalizing, Cut Flowers, Foliage, Seed heads, Flowers attractive to bees and butterflies;* and for tolerance of: *Coastal and Inland exposure, Air pollution, Garden pests.*

SPECIFIC USES

FLORAL EFFECT

For flowers throughout the year and for different uses and effects, this section suggests perennials in the following categories: *Long flowering season; Spring, Early to midsummer, Mid- to late summer, Autumn, or Winter flowering; Flowers borne in sprays and flattened heads, or spikes; Hot-, Cool-, or Pale-coloured flowers; Fragrant flowers.*

FOLIAGE EFFECT

Foliage forms the basis of any garden. Perennials in this section are grouped by their leaf type: *Bold, Evergreen, Strap- or sword-shaped, Deep-cut or jagged, Feathery, Spiny, Aromatic, Yellow- or gold-variegated, White- or cream-variegated, Gold, Silver or grey-blue, Purple, red, or bronze, Richly tinted in autumn, Decorative in winter.*

FLORAL EFFECT

FOLIAGE EFFECT

SPECIALIST PLANTS

Some perennials are particularly sought after for their form, foliage, or flowers. This section includes families of perennials that are often collected by enthusiasts: *Geraniums, Hostas, Snowdrops, Hellebores, Epimediums, Peonies.* Some of these plant groups also make excellent specimen plants: *Bamboos, Small grasses and sedges, Large grasses, Ferns.*

SPECIALIST PLANTS

AGM ♔ ●
Shows the plant has received an RHS Award of Garden Merit.

PLANTS WITH A SEAL OF APPROVAL

The Royal Horticultural Society gives an Award of Garden Merit to plants whose decorative effect, good constitution, ease of care and cultivation, and availability is excellent. It identifies some of the best species and cultivars available. The AGM symbol is often displayed on plants in garden centres.

♔   *Award of Garden Merit*

INTRODUCTION

PERENNIALS FOUND GROWING in wild meadows, forests, and coastal or mountainous regions all over the world have long made a valuable contribution to our gardens. The most varied and versatile of plants, they are easy to grow and will bring year-round attractions of foliage and flowers to gardens of any size and situation.

△ AUTHOR'S GARDEN *Many perennials flourish alongside shrubs and trees in my own garden in Hampshire.*

Coreopsis 'Moonbeam' for pale-coloured flowers

The earliest images I have of garden perennials are the ragged blue heads of perennial cornflowers (*Centaurea montana*) growing in my grandfather's garden when I was a boy. Little did I know then that one day, not only would I travel through the world's wild places in search of native plants, but I would also make gardening my career. In the years since, I have come to recognize and know perennials in the wild in a great variety of situations, from mountain woods and meadows to coastal plains and swamps. Seeing them in their natural habitats where they choose to grow, as well as in gardens where we want them to grow, has taught me a lot about their needs, their preferences, and their huge garden potential. Contrary to what we

WHY GROW PERENNIALS?

Variety and versatility are the two main benefits that perennials bring to the garden. There isn't a single garden site in which perennials of some kind cannot be grown. Used with shrubs and trees to build a coherent garden structure, they can provide ground cover, form the bulk of border plants, or fill containers. They offer gardeners year-round colour and interest with their vast range of foliage and flower effects, seed heads, and scents. Most are easily cultivated in temperate regions, and can be increased by sowing seed, taking cuttings, or division.

Helleborus argutifolius for evergreen leaves

◁ NATURAL HABITAT *Perennials in the wild give us a number of clues about how we can best use them in our gardens, and may also inform and inspire our choice of garden design. This alpine meadow in China's Yunnan province contains many perennials that can be grown in a sunny scree or rock garden in cultivation.*

might expect, the situations and soils in which perennials are found in the wild are not always those that they demand in the garden, although they do offer us some important basic guidelines.

ADAPTABLE AND VERSATILE

Perennials are surprisingly adaptable in cultivation and will tolerate a variety of conditions, with only the inevitable exceptions to this rule, such as those requiring lime-free soil, calling for special care and attention. Temperature requirements are another matter, however, for it stands to reason that those perennials growing naturally in warm climates, especially those that enjoy hot, sunny, well-drained conditions, will not thrive in cold gardens where the sun rarely visits. Nevertheless, many enterprising gardeners in such situations have devised ways of circumventing the problem, taking advantage of sheltered corners to grow tender or exotic perennials, or planting in containers that can be moved indoors or under glass when inclement weather threatens.

IN THE GARDEN

In my own garden in Hampshire, on a soil that is mainly sandy and free-draining, I now grow many

hundreds of perennials, as well as trees and shrubs. Drawing on this practical experience of perennials in cultivation, and in the wild, I have tried in *What Perennial Where* to suggest some of the best plants for given soils and situations, as well as providing information on their ornamental merits and utility value. If this book helps you to grow a plant where once there was nothing, then I shall have succeeded.

△ ATTRACTIVE GROUND COVER *Many low-growing or mat-forming perennials provide good ground cover. Often thriving in shade, they are also ideal for softening the edges of borders, paths, or steps, or for underplanting beneath shrubs and trees.*

▽ BRIGHT BORDER *Still one of the most popular uses of perennials in the garden, the herbaceous border, devised in the late 19th century, formally arranges plants by height, and often by flower colour.*

Designing with Perennials

COLOUR, FORM, AND TEXTURE all play an important role in garden design, and perennials offer the widest choice of these ingredients. A designed garden may include particular features, such as water or paving, or follow a theme, whether historical, low in allergens, or in colour or mood. By knowing which perennials are best suited to your plans, they can be used creatively to enhance any scheme.

Space, climate, soil, and aspect are all factors that may influence your choice of garden design and the plants best suited to your needs. In most situations there is a huge range of perennials to choose from for optimum effect, although problem sites, such as boggy areas, coastal gardens, or clay soil, will all require at least some specialized plants tolerant of such conditions. It is worth remembering that form and foliage are just as important, if not more so, than flowers. They provide the garden with a firm basis on which to build, and also establish a long-lasting backdrop for whatever flowers briefly appear. While many perennials have richly tinted leaves in autumn, there are others that have the advantage of a longer display of variegated, coloured, or even evergreen foliage.

PERENNIAL PLANTING

With the exception of ground cover schemes and some formal designs, it is vital to maintain enough space between perennials grown in beds, borders, and screes. This allows for expansion and also the possibility of self-sown seedlings, which may even result in new forms or hybrids. Group plants that enjoy similar growing conditions together, and

△ MIXED TUB *Containers are ideal for patios or small gardens where space is at a premium. Perennials with attractive leaves, like* Houttuynia, Heuchera, *and* Tolmiea, *are striking and long-lasting.*

▷ GRAND DESIGNS *The spectacular borders of landscaped gardens are a good source of ideas. Height or colour contrasts are easy to repeat on a smaller scale.*

▽ TEXTURE AND COLOUR *The different habits, foliage, and flowers of* Melissa, Linaria, *and* Geranium *'Johnson's Blue' create a vibrant and informal display.*

△ COLOUR SPECTRUM *It is possible to achieve impressive effects without using a vast array of perennials. Different forms of the same or similar plants, as in this* Sedum *border, can be planted together to make a bold display.*

△ NATURAL PLANTING *Drifts of grasses and other perennials create an informal effect in this border, inspired by plants in the wild. This increasingly popular style of gardening uses plants appropriate to the site for a low-maintenance approach.*

select perennials best suited to the soil and aspect of your garden to ensure strong, healthy growth and easy management.

GARDEN DESIGNS

Large, landscaped gardens show the scope for spectacular design and the wealth of planting possible where space is no object. However, if scale and contrast are taken into consideration, the grand herbaceous perennial borders often found in these settings can inspire gardeners of even the smallest plots. Small groups of compact plants can easily be combined to recreate the foliage or flowering effects seen in larger beds. Alternatively, try using a single large plant as a highlight. Containers are also a useful option, particularly for small gardens, back-yards, or patios. Bamboos, ferns, and many other foliage and flowering perennials are ideal for containers, and there is a good selection of shade-lovers that will thrive even in sunless areas near to the house.

The "plantsman's garden", where individual plants take precedence over rigid design, will appeal to those gardeners wanting to establish a collection of specialist perennials. While plant variety is the most important consideration here, careful planning of paths and beds will help you cope more easily with the garden's contents.

NATURAL EFFECTS

"Wild" plantings look to perennials growing in their natural habitats for inspiration. Where space allows, the effect of natural woodland,

water features, or meadows can be recreated in the garden. Variety is not of prime importance in the wild garden, and large numbers of a few key perennials can be planted in sweeping drifts, naturalized in isolation, or underplanted beneath trees or shrubs. The plants chosen must be tolerant of competition, especially if planted in grass or shade, which is why many bulbs, or robust clump-forming or fast-creeping perennials, are ideal for this purpose.

An increasingly popular variation on the wild garden is "natural" planting. This involves planting whole borders or beds with loose drifts of perennials, including ornamental grasses. There is no place here for the ordered blocks or tight groups of plants found in more formal designs, as these natural-style borders emulate the

effects found in meadows and prairies in the wild. Depending on your taste, or on the size of your garden, it is possible to incorporate just a few grasses into a compact border of perennials or, in larger gardens where space is no object, to create wilder, more naturalistic sweeps of plants. Part of the success of this style of planting is that it uses perennials appropriate to the chosen site. The result is a low-maintenance, wildlife-friendly garden, where plants thrive and care for themselves with less need for intervention such as staking, watering, or pest control.

FACTORS TO CONSIDER WHEN DESIGNING WITH PERENNIALS

Light Where and when shade occurs in your garden is critical as this affects your choice of perennials for different sites. Many perennials tolerate shade; others need all the sun they can get.

Hardiness Give priority to perennials best suited to your local conditions. In colder regions, tender or more exotic perennials may survive in warm, sheltered pockets or in containers.

Colour and texture Flowers are the most obvious providers of colour in the garden, but often appear only briefly. Perennials with attractive foliage offer valuable texture and drama as well as year-round interest.

Structure Exploit diversity in growth habits and plant size to give structure to formal schemes, such as herbaceous borders, or to fulfil specific functions such as ground cover or screening.

Naturalizing Many perennials (bulbs especially) are spectacular planted in drifts for natural effect, particularly in wild, marginal areas. Use them also beneath deciduous shrubs or roses.

Additional uses Many perennials have imposing foliage and flowerheads, some good for cutting, which make them ideal specimen plants. They can also be used to complement walls, paths, or other architectural features.

Perennials through the Seasons

EACH SEASON has its own particular character and brings new features to the garden landscape. Perennials mirror this seasonal passage by offering continual changes in growth, foliage, and flowers. While spring and summer are often considered to be the high points of the gardening calendar, with careful thought and positive planting perennials can provide year-round interest and colourful or dramatic effects, with one plant taking over as another starts to fade.

Seasonal changes in the garden are reflected most clearly in flowering and foliage displays. While some perennials flower for only a comparatively brief period, their spectacular blooms may be long remembered and eagerly looked forward to in subsequent years. Other perennials with extended flowering, often spanning several months, provide strong links between the seasons, and their contribution can be relied upon year after year. This is particularly important in smaller gardens, where each plant must justify its place in the planting scheme. Perennials with attractive foliage will provide an even longer season of interest, and can be invaluable where space is limited. While herbaceous plants often have richly tinted leaves in autumn, it is worth planting some of the many perennials that have evergreen, brightly coloured, or variegated foliage for longer-lasting colour and texture in the garden.

SPRING

The re-emergence of herbaceous perennials in spring is, for many gardeners, one of the most exciting events in the year. Rootstocks that have lain below ground all through winter now send out strong, and sometimes brightly coloured, new shoots. As many trees and shrubs are slower to produce new growth in spring, perennials provide much of the first garden colour of the new year. Bulbs will bring welcome early blooms and are excellent for planting in groups, naturalizing in large drifts, or underplanting beneath trees or shrubs. Tulips,

△ SPRING CONTAINER *Bulbs, like these* Narcissus, *are ideal for naturalizing or for tubs. They are a useful source of early colour in the garden, providing a rich variety of spring flower effects.*

▷ SUMMER BORDER *Perennials can bring a blaze of colour to the garden during the summer months. In this border, the bright blooms of delphiniums, lupins,* Anthemis, Oenothera, *and* Geranium psilostemon *compete with a multitude of other plants for our attention.*

△ EARLY WINTER *After flowering, many perennials produce decorative seed heads. These can provide enchanting effects when gilded with hoar frost, a bonus that tidy-minded gardeners often forfeit.*

◁ AUTUMN COLOUR *The richly tinted foliage of* Geranium macrorrhizum *is a striking backdrop for colchicums in autumn. The leaf colour will continue to develop after the flowers have faded.*

daffodils, and many other bulbs can also provide some of the first cut flowers of the year, and will thrive in containers on a patio.

SUMMER

After the initial rush of spring flowers, the garden settles down to a more leisurely pace. Many of our most popular border perennials, such as *Achillea*, *Heliopsis*, *Inula*, and other members of the huge daisy family are at their best now. Long-flowering perennials, like *Oenothera*, will bloom throughout summer and even on into autumn. Summer is also the time when perennials with a stately habit or bold foliage attain their ultimate size, stamping their presence on the garden scene. In areas where summers are dry, it is worth growing perennials such as eryngiums and yuccas, which will tolerate hot sun and little water.

AUTUMN

Perennials with late flowers, fruits, or richly tinted foliage can make autumn one of the most colourful seasons, despite its place at the end

of the growing year. Autumn bulbs, such as colchicums and dwarf cyclamen, flower alongside golden rod (*Solidago*) and michaelmas daisies (*Aster*). Foliage can also make an important contribution – the dying leaves of herbaceous perennials such as *Geranium wlassovianum* providing brilliant tints of purple, yellow, and red to accompany the bright seed heads, often good for cutting, borne by many other plants. Wise gardeners will also use ornamental grasses, like the striking pampas grass (*Cortaderia selloana*), to add interest to borders or containers. In addition to their bold form and foliage, many of these grasses have striking seed heads that will last into winter.

WINTER

The winter months are often least liked by gardeners, but this does not have to be a featureless time

▷ MID-WINTER *Use perennials to bring warmth and colour to the winter garden. Here,* Bergenia *'Bressingham Ruby' provides a lovely foil for some snowdrops.*

when the garden is either ignored or avoided. Numerous perennials, including bamboos, have attractive overwintering or evergreen foliage, some of it brightly coloured. These foliage plants, invaluable in their own right, will also provide a setting for mid- to late-winter-flowering pulmonarias and hellebores, as well as for snowdrops and other similar miniature bulbs that signal the oncoming spring. Perennials whose dried superstructures or seed heads survive through autumn into winter will provide further beauty and dramatic interest in the garden.

SOIL AND ASPECT

THE TYPE OF SOIL found in your garden and how much sun or shade it enjoys are two of the most critical factors to consider when selecting plants for your plot. While many perennials are flexible in their needs, tolerating a range of garden situations, they can be used to better effect if you are aware of their preferences.

Anemonopsis macrophylla
for moist soil in shade

Soils vary considerably in their physical and chemical nature, and while most perennials thrive on what is commonly called average or "moist but well-drained" soil, which retains enough moisture to satisfy a plant's needs without becoming waterlogged, some have more specific requirements. Look at the colour and texture of your soil and use the soil panel (*right*) to establish which type of soil you have.

All plants require some sunlight to survive, but while some demand full sun for top performance, others tolerate, or even prefer, varying degrees of shade. Many perennials thrive in the partial shade cast by buildings, walls, or light-canopied deciduous trees, like birch. A more careful choice of plants is needed, however, for sites in the heavy shade found beneath dense, and especially evergreen, tree canopies.

Perennials in this section are grouped according to their soil and lighting needs to provide planting solutions for a range of garden sites.

SOIL GUIDE

The clay, sand, or silt particles in your garden soil will dictate its physical and chemical make-up. It may be heavy (wet and poorly drained) or light (dry and free-draining). Acidity or alkalinity (pH value) is measured on a scale of 1 to 14. Below neutral (7), soils are acid; above neutral they are alkaline (limy).

AVERAGE *soil suits the widest range of plants. Slightly acid or neutral, it is moist but well-drained.*

HEAVY CLAY *soil can be very fertile, but its tiny particles make it slow-draining if wet, and hard-baked if dry.*

SANDY *soil has large particles and is light and free-draining. It often loses nutrients and water quickly.*

LIME-FREE *or peat soil is acid and often rich in organic matter. It is dark in colour and retains moisture.*

ALKALINE *or limy soil (including chalk) is pale, shallow, and stony. Free-draining, it is fairly fertile.*

△ SHADY BORDER *Many perennials, like these hostas and irises, enjoy a partially shady site, especially if the soil is moist.*

◁ SUNNY CORNER *Make use of warm, sheltered sites and corners to grow sun-loving, tender, or more exotic perennials.*

▷ DRY GARDEN *These striking sedums, eryngiums, and ornamental grasses will thrive in full sun and a well-drained soil.*

Low to Medium Perennials for Heavy Clay Soil

OTHER LOW TO MEDIUM GROWERS FOR HEAVY CLAY SOIL

Astilbe 'Rheinland'
Astrantia major 'Shaggy', see p.100
Brunnera macrophylla, see p.78
Polemonium 'Lambrook Mauve', see p.79
Primula denticulata
Prunella grandiflora
Stachys macrantha, see p.93
Thermopsis rhombifolia, see p.79
Veronica gentianoides

HEAVY CLAY SOILS can be wet and sticky in winter, but hard and lumpy in dry summers. They can also be, when well worked and mulched, fertile and amenable to the cultivation of a wide range of perennials. None of the following will grow much above 90cm (36in), and are suited to small gardens, or the front of larger borders and beds.

Ajuga reptans 'Multicolor'
COMMON BUGLE
☼ ❄❄❄ ↕15cm (6in) ↔ 90cm (36in)

This bugle forms a dense, evergreen mat of creeping stems and bronze-green leaves splashed pink and cream. Short spikes of deep blue flowers open in early summer.

Aster x *frikartii* 'Mönch'
ASTER
☼ ❄❄❄ ↕70cm (28in) ↔ 40cm (16in)

Well worth growing for its reliable display of big, long-lasting, lavender-blue daisies, borne on strong stems in late summer and autumn. It may require support.

Campanula takesimana
BELLFLOWER
☼ ☼ ❄❄❄ ↕50cm (20in) ↔ 1m (3ft)

Reliable on clay soils, this suckering plant has erect stems and heart-shaped leaves. Nodding white bell-flowers, pink-flushed and spotted within, are borne in summer.

Aquilegia vulgaris 'Nora Barlow'
GRANNY'S BONNET
☼ ☼ ❄❄❄ ↕90cm (36in) ↔ 45cm (18in)

During spring and early summer, tall, erect stems produce showers of nodding, pale green and red pompon flowers above a mound of prettily divided leaves.

Bergenia crassifolia
ELEPHANT'S EAR
☼ ☼ ❄❄❄ ↕↔45cm (18in)

A tough perennial, developing a mound of bold, leathery, evergreen leaves. Reddish stems carry dark pink flowers above the foliage during late winter and early spring.

Hemerocallis 'Stella de Oro'
DAYLILY
☼ ❄❄❄ ↕30cm (12in) ↔ 45cm (18in)

During early summer, clusters of bright yellow flowers open in succession above the dense, low clump of strap-shaped, semi-evergreen leaves. It is very reliable.

Hosta 'June'
PLANTAIN LILY
☼ ☀ ❄❄❄ ↕ 40cm (16in) ↔ 70cm (28in)

This beautiful foliage plant is a sport of
the lovely *H.* 'Halcyon'. It has fleshy,
long-pointed, yellow-splashed leaves and
bears lavender-grey flowers in summer.

Lamium orvala
DEAD NETTLE
☼ ☀ ❄❄❄ ↕↔ 50cm (20in)

The softly-hairy, nettle-shaped leaves
form a bold, non-invasive clump. Whorls
of two-lipped, pinkish purple flowers are
produced from late spring into summer.

Paeonia 'Laura Dessert'
PEONY
☼ ❄❄❄ ↕ 75cm (30in) ↔ 60cm (24in)

In early summer, large, fragrant, double,
creamy yellow blooms, with pink-flushed
outer petals, are borne above a bold clump
of deeply divided, light green leaves. 🏆

Ranunculus aconitifolius 'Flore Pleno'
FAIR MAIDS OF KENT
☼ ☀ ❄❄❄ ↕ 60cm (24in) ↔ 45cm (18in)

Old-fashioned and very popular, this has
beautiful, deeply lobed leaves and bears
branched stems of double white button
flowers in spring and early summer. 🏆

Prunella grandiflora 'Loveliness'
SELF-HEAL
☼ ❄❄❄ ↕ 15cm (6in) ↔ 30cm (12in)

A mat-forming, semi-evergreen perennial
with erect stems bearing whorled heads of
two-lipped, soft pink flowers in summer.
It will provide good ground cover.

Rudbeckia fulgida var. *sullivantii*
'Goldsturm'
☼ ☀ ❄❄❄ ↕ 60cm (24in) ↔ 45cm (18in)

As long as it is kept moist in summer, this
colourful perennial is reliable. Its large,
dark-centred, golden yellow daisy-heads
open from late summer into autumn. 🏆

Medium to Tall Perennials for Heavy Clay Soil

MANY OF THE MORE ROBUST perennials are tolerant of heavy clay soils. Some have densely fibrous rootstocks, others are deep-rooted, allowing them to survive so long as their site is not waterlogged. The following perennials, all 1–2m (3–6ft) tall, will do even better in these conditions if drainage can be improved by adding coarse grit and compost.

Delphinium 'Emily Hawkins'
DELPHINIUM
☼ ✳✳✳ ↕ 1.7m (5½ft) ↔ 60cm (24in)

No perennial border on clay soil should be without a delphinium. This one produces neat, semi-double, light violet flowers, with fawn-coloured eyes, in summer. ♈

Aconitum × *cammarum* 'Bicolor'
MONKSHOOD
☼ ☼ ✳✳✳ ↕ 1.2m (4ft) ↔ 60cm (24in)

This stout perennial has deeply divided, sharply toothed, dark green leaves and bears branched heads of helmet-shaped, blue and white flowers during summer. ♈

Centaurea macrocephala
CENTAUREA
☼ ✳✳✳ ↕ 1.5m (5ft) ↔ 90cm (36in)

Throughout summer, large, chunky heads of golden yellow cornflowers, with shiny brown bracts, top the erect, leafy stems of this striking, clump-forming perennial.

Aruncus dioicus
GOATSBEARD
☼ ☼ ✳✳✳ ↕ 2m (6ft) ↔ 1.2m (4ft)

An impressive perennial forming a bold clump of large, much-divided, fern-like leaves, with equally attractive plumes of frothy, creamy white summer flowers. ♈

Cimicifuga simplex 'Scimitar'
BUGBANE
☼ ☼ ✳✳✳ ↕ 2m (6ft) ↔ 60cm (24in)

A handsome perennial with tall, branched spikes of tiny white flowers that rise over the large, bold clumps of deeply divided, fern-like leaves during autumn.

Eupatorium purpureum
'Atropurpureum'
☼ ✳✳✳ ↕ 2.2m (7ft) ↔ 1.2m (4ft)

The dense, domed heads of pink-purple flowers, loved by butterflies and bees, are borne by stout, erect clumps of purplish, tall, leafy stems in summer and autumn.

Helianthus 'Capenoch Star'
PERENNIAL SUNFLOWER
☼ ☀ ❄❄❄ ↕ 1.5m (5ft) ↔ 90cm (36in)

The sharply toothed leaves of this bold, clump-forming plant are joined in summer and autumn by branched heads of large, lemon-yellow, dark-centred daisies. ♈

Heliopsis helianthoides subsp. *scabra*
'Light of Loddon'
☼ ☀ ❄❄❄ ↕ 1.1m (3½ft) ↔ 90cm (36in)

During summer and autumn, the erect, stout, stiff-branching, leafy stems produce a regular display of semi-double, bright yellow flowerheads with domed centres.

OTHER MEDIUM TO TALL PERENNIALS FOR CLAY SOIL

Persicaria amplexicaulis 'Firetail'
PERSICARIA
☼ ☀ ❄❄❄ ↕ 1.2m (4ft) ↔ 90cm (36in)

A striking and reliable border perennial, with dense clumps of leafy stems bearing long, arching, slender spikes of bright red flowers from summer into autumn. ♈

Rodgersia aesculifolia
RODGERSIA
☼ ☀ ❄❄❄ ↕ 1.7m (5½ft) ↔ 90cm (36in)

This lovely rodgersia produces a clump of long-stalked, toothed, horse-chestnut-like leaves, topped by bold plumes of creamy white flowers during summer. ♈

Silphium perfoliatum
PRAIRIE DOCK
☼ ☀ ❄❄❄ ↕ 2.5m (8ft) ↔ 1m (3ft)

Branched heads of yellow daisy-flowers adorn this statuesque plant in summer and autumn. The stalks of the coarse-toothed upper leaves are fused, forming cups.

Low to Medium Perennials for Sandy/Free-draining Soil

THERE ARE NUMEROUS PERENNIALS less than 1m (3ft) in height that are suitable for well-drained soils, especially those benefiting from full sun. These small plants have a multitude of uses, particularly at the front of borders, in raised beds, or on the tops of walls. Some are also excellent for growing in containers on patios or paved areas.

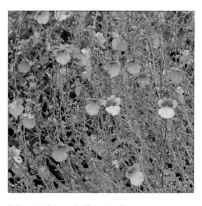

Diascia 'Joyce's Choice'
DIASCIA
☼ ❄❄   ↕ 25cm (10in) ↔ 50cm (20in)

A free-flowering diascia, forming a mat or carpet of trailing stems and small leaves, topped throughout summer and autumn by loose sprays of apricot flowers. ♔

Acanthus hirsutus
ACANTHUS
☼ ◐ ❄❄❄   ↕↔ 30cm (12in)

This low, suckering perennial forms a clump or patch of deep-cut, weakly spiny leaves. In summer, erect, greenish white flower spikes emerge from prickly bracts.

Artemisia 'Powis Castle'
ARTEMISIA
☼ ❄❄   ↕ 60cm (24in) ↔ 90cm (36in)

The filigree, silvery grey foliage of this plant is hard to beat. It forms a low, neat mound, eventually becoming woody and untidy, when it should be replaced. ♔

Eriophyllum lanatum
WOOLLY SUNFLOWER
☼ ❄❄❄   ↕↔ 50cm (20in)

This vigorous clump-former has woolly, silvery grey leaves and bears a succession of bright yellow daisy-flowers from late spring into summer. It is drought-tolerant.

Agapanthus 'Midnight Blue'
SOUTH AFRICAN LILY
☼ ❄❄❄   ↕ 45cm (18in) ↔ 30cm (12in)

In summer, fleshy stems rise from the clump of strap-shaped, dark green leaves to carry loose heads of dark blue trumpet-flowers. It is very reliable in most gardens.

Borago pygmaea
BORAGO
☼ ❄❄❄   ↕↔ 60cm (24in)

A short-lived plant, with loosely branched stems rising from rosettes of leaves. Pale blue, nodding bell-flowers emerge over a long period from early summer to autumn.

Eryngium bourgatii
ERYNGIUM
☼ ❄❄❄   ↕ 45cm (18in) ↔ 30cm (12in)

Small blue flowerheads, with collars of spine-tipped bracts, open in summer on branching stems. The spiny, silver-veined, deeply divided leaves form rosettes. ♔

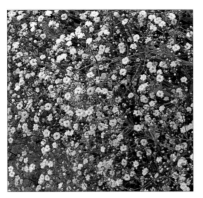

Gypsophila 'Rosenschleier'
GYPSOPHILA
☼ ❄❄❄   ↕ 40cm (16in) ↔ 1m (3ft)

The pretty carpet of bluish green leaves is
peppered in summer with tiny, double
white flowers, which later turn pale pink.
It is also known as *G.* 'Rosy Veil'. ♔

Limonium latifolium 'Violetta'
SEA LAVENDER
☼ ❄❄❄   ↕ 60cm (24in) ↔ 45cm (18in)

This sea lavender forms a bold rosette of
large, dark green leaves. Branched heads
of tiny, deep bluish violet, late-summer
flowers are good for cutting and drying.

Oenothera speciosa 'Rosea'
OENOTHERA
☼ ❄❄❄   ↕↔ 30cm (12in)

From early summer to autumn, saucer-
shaped, pale pink blooms, with yellow and
white centres, decorate the hummock of
narrow leaves. Free- and long-flowering.

Linum narbonense
LINUM
☼ ❄❄❄   ↕ 50cm (20in) ↔ 45cm (18in)

In summer, clumps of slender, wiry stems,
clothed in narrow, blue-green leaves, bear
a mass of short-lived, white-eyed blue
flowers. A relative of the flax or linseed.

OTHER LOW TO MEDIUM GROWERS FOR SANDY/FREE-DRAINING SOIL

Acanthus dioscoridis, see p.26
Agastache 'Firebird'
Allium cristophii, see p.26
Anagallis monellii
Ballota 'All Hallows Green'
Centranthus ruber, see p.86
Delphinium tatsienense, see p.26
Dianthus deltoides, see p.100
Dictamnus albus, see p.108
Euphorbia nicaeensis, see p.76
Euphorbia rigida
Geranium 'Brookside', see p.27
Geranium malviflorum
Hordeum jubatum
Iris innominata
Lychnis coronaria
Origanum laevigatum
Pulsatilla vulgaris f. *alba*, see p.27

Origanum laevigatum 'Herrenhausen'
OREGANO
☼ ❄❄❄   ↕ 50cm (20in) ↔ 45cm (18in)

Bees and butterflies love this plant. The
stiffly erect stems, crowded with aromatic
leaves, are topped by dense heads of rich
pink flowers in summer and autumn. ♔

Medium to Tall Perennials for Sandy/Free-draining Soil

EVERGREEN, MEDIUM TO TALL GROWERS FOR SANDY SOIL

Acanthus mollis Latifolius Group
Cortaderia selloana
  'Sunningdale Silver', see p.139
Dierama pulcherrimum 'Blackbird'
Eryngium yuccifolium
Euphorbia characias subsp. *wulfenii*
Lavatera 'Barnsley', see p.28
Phormium tenax, see p.117
Salvia interrupta
Yucca whipplei

THOSE OF YOU WHO HAVE ADMIRED the huge mound of a *Crambe cordifolia* in bloom, or the lavender-blue spires of a *Perovskia*, may already know how well these two, and other similar perennials, thrive in well-drained soil, especially in sunny sites. The following, mostly 1–2m (3–6ft) tall, also enjoy such conditions, and will bring presence to a border or bed.

Asphodeline lutea
KING'S SPEAR
☼ ✽✽✽   ↕ 1.5m (5ft) ↔ 30cm (12in)

Well named, as the slender spikes of starry yellow flowers, borne above the clumps of grassy, blue-grey leaves in summer, really do have the appearance of golden spears.

Crambe cordifolia
CRAMBE
☼ ☼ ✽✽✽   ↕ 2.5m (8ft) ↔ 1.5m (5ft)

Truly imposing when in full bloom, the tiny, pure white flowers are borne in huge, branching heads above mounds of bold, dark green foliage in early summer. 🏆

Echinops bannaticus 'Taplow Blue'
GLOBE THISTLE
☼ ☼ ✽✽✽   ↕ 1.2m (4ft) ↔ 60cm (24in)

The prickly balls of bright blue flowers in mid- to late summer make this a favourite with both children and butterflies. It has handsome, deep-cut, spiny leaves. 🏆

Cortaderia selloana 'Rendatleri'
PINK PAMPAS GRASS
☼ ✽✽✽   ↕ 2.5m (8ft) ↔ 2m (6ft)

A favourite pampas grass, with a huge pile of narrow, saw-toothed, evergreen leaves, and tall stems flaunting bold plumes of rosy lilac spikelets during late summer.

Dierama pulcherrimum
WANDFLOWER
☼ ✽✽   ↕ 1.5m (5ft) ↔ 1.2m (4ft)

Known also as angel's fishing rod, because of its graceful, arching stems hung with magenta-pink or purple bell-flowers in summer. Its seed heads are attractive too.

Eryngium eburneum
ERYNGIUM
☼ ✽✽   ↕ 4m (12ft) ↔ 2m (6ft)

This statuesque plant bears tall-stemmed, branching heads of white-green flowers in summer, above bold clumps of rapier-like, spine-toothed, evergreen leaves.

Kniphofia 'Prince Igor'
TORCH LILY
☀ ☀ ✳✳✳ ↕ 1.8m (6ft) ↔ 90cm (36in)

This is an outstanding kniphofia, bearing narrow, rich green leaves, and numerous sturdy stems with large, dense pokers of deep orange-red flowers during autumn.

Linaria dalmatica
TOADFLAX
☀ ✳✳✳ ↕ ↔ 90cm (36in)

Bushy with a creeping rootstock, this toadflax has erect stems crowded with bloomy, blue-green leaves. Long spikes of yellow snapdragon flowers open during summer.

HERBACEOUS, MEDIUM TO TALL
GROWERS FOR SANDY SOIL

Echinops ritro 'Veitch's Blue', see p.73
Echinops sphaerocephalus
Eremurus robustus, see p.28
Eremurus stenophyllus, see p.33
Lilium chalcedonicum
Lilium regale, see p.110
Malva alcea var. *fastigiata*, see p.93
Salvia involucrata 'Bethellii'
Verbascum chaixii 'Album',
    see p.103

Romneya coulteri
MATILIJA
☀ ✳✳ ↕ ↔ 2m (6ft)

A suckering, woody-based perennial or subshrub, in time forming patches of sea-green, bloomy, leafy stems. In summer, it bears large, yellow-centred flowers. ♛

Salvia cacaliifolia
ORNAMENTAL SAGE
☀ ✳✳✳ ↕ 1.2m (4ft) ↔ 90cm (36in)

A robust, branching, hairy perennial with triangular leaves, and slender sprays of deep blue flowers from midsummer to autumn. It needs a warm, sunny site. ♛

Lavatera 'Kew Rose'
TREE MALLOW
☀ ✳✳ ↕ ↔ 2m (6ft)

Deservedly popular, this mallow produces branching, woody-based stems of semi-evergreen leaves, and a succession of pink flowers in summer. Likes a sheltered spot.

Perovskia 'Blue Spire'
RUSSIAN SAGE
☀ ✳✳✳ ↕ 1.2m (4ft) ↔ 90cm (36in)

This drought-tolerant, aromatic, woody-based sage has erect, downy stems, and branched spires of flowers in summer and autumn. Herbaceous in cold winters. ♛

Verbascum 'Gainsborough'
MULLEIN
☀ ✳✳✳ ↕ 1.2m (4ft) ↔ 30cm (12in)

Beautiful but short-lived, this mullein has downy, wrinkled leaves in attractive, over-wintering rosettes. Branched spires of soft yellow flowers appear in summer. ♛

Low-growing Perennials for Lime-free Soil

WHILE THE NUMBER OF PLANTS that demand lime-free conditions for successful cultivation is small compared with those that do not, the category includes some of the loveliest and most desirable of perennials. The perennials below will not grow much above 30cm (12in), making them suitable for rock gardens or for small peat gardens and beds.

Celmisia walkeri
NEW ZEALAND DAISY
☼ ☼ ❋❋❋   ↕ ↔ 30cm (12in)

This mat-forming, evergreen perennial or subshrub has rosettes of leathery, greyish leaves, and white, yellow-centred daisies borne on sticky stems in early summer.

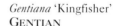

Gentiana 'Kingfisher'
GENTIAN
☼ ☼ ❋❋❋   ↕ 5cm (2in) ↔ 30cm (12in)

In autumn, beautiful trumpet-shaped blue flowers, with white and darker blue stripes on the outside, are borne among the semi-evergreen mats of rosetted, narrow leaves.

Dodecatheon meadia f. *album*
SHOOTING STAR
☼ ☼ ❋❋❋   ↕ 40cm (16in) ↔ 25cm (10in)

In spring, this exquisite plant bears loose umbels of nodding, pure white flowers, with yellow beaks of stamens, on slender stems above a basal rosette of leaves. ♈

Iris 'Arnold Sunrise'
PACIFIC COAST IRIS
☼ ☼ ❋❋❋   ↕ 25cm (10in) ↔ 30cm (12in)

A tough, clump-forming plant, forming patches of long, narrow, evergreen leaves. Erect stems bear yellow-stained white flowers in spring. Will tolerate dry soil. ♈

Lithodora diffusa 'Grace Ward'
LITHODORA
☼ ❋❋❋   ↕ 15cm (6in) ↔ 90cm (36in)

Deep azure-blue flowers top the prostrate, leafy stems of this dense, carpeting, evergreen perennial or subshrub in late spring and summer. Ideal for rock gardens. ♈

Medium to Tall Perennials for Lime-free Soil

T HE FOLLOWING PERENNIALS all perform best in lime-free, preferably acid conditions. Many are natives of woodland and mountain sites and require some moisture in spring and summer (but not waterlogged soil) in order to thrive. They will grow to around 1m (3ft) tall, and provide superb displays of foliage and flowers for a bed or garden with peaty soil.

Meconopsis chelidoniifolia
MECONOPSIS
☀ ✳✳✳   ↕ 1m (3ft) ↔ 60cm (24in)

Elegant yet informal, this plant develops clumps of leafy, slender, semi-scandent, branching stems. Nodding, saucer-shaped, pale yellow flowers are borne in summer.

Blechnum tabulare
BLECHNUM
☀ ☀ ✳✳✳   ↕ 1m (3ft) ↔ 1.2m (4ft)

This large, evergreen fern forms a bold clump of laddered, leathery, sterile fronds. Stiff, fertile fronds crowded with brown spore clusters rise from the centre. ♉

Thalictrum rochebruneanum
MEADOW RUE
☀ ✳✳✳   ↕ 90cm (36in) ↔ 30cm (12in)

A stately, upright perennial with clumps of large, much-divided, fern-like leaves and tall stems. Fluffy, white or lavender-pink flower clusters are borne in summer.

Iris ensata 'Variegata'
IRIS
☀ ✳✳✳   ↕ 90cm (36in) ↔ 45cm (18in)

In summer, this clump-forming iris bears dark red-purple flowers on erect stems above its upright, sword-shaped, striped, greyish green leaves. Enjoys moist soils.

Lilium auratum
GOLDEN-RAYED LILY
☀ ☀ ✳✳✳   ↕ 1.5 (5ft) ↔ 30cm (12in)

Tall stems, crowded with lance-shaped leaves, each bear up to 12 large white blooms, speckled crimson and striped gold, in late summer and early autumn.

> **OTHER MEDIUM TO TALL PERENNIALS FOR LIME-FREE SOIL**
>
> *Iris ensata*
> *Iris ensata* 'Rose Queen'
> *Meconopsis betonicifolia*
> *Meconopsis grandis*
> *Meconopsis × sheldonii* 'Slieve Donard'
> *Megacarpaea polyandra*
> *Nomocharis pardanthina*
> *Osmunda regalis,* see p.61
> *Thalictrum chelidonii*
> *Thalictrum diffusiflorum*

Low to Medium Perennials for Alkaline Soil

CONTRARY TO THE BELIEF of some gardeners that many of the choicest garden plants demand lime-free soil, more perennials in fact thrive on, rather than dislike, alkaline conditions. None of the following will grow to more than 1m (3ft) high and are therefore suitable for the front of borders, as well as for raised beds and rock gardens.

Bergenia 'Beethoven'
ELEPHANT'S EAR
☼ ☼ ✳✳✳ ↕ 45cm (18in) ↔ 60cm (24in)

This fine hybrid of German origin forms a low clump of bold, leathery leaves, above which loose heads of white flowers with reddish calyces are borne in spring.

Acanthus dioscoridis
ACANTHUS
☼ ✳✳✳ ↕ 40cm (16in) ↔ 60cm (24in)

A striking relative of *A. mollis*, forming clumps of lance-shaped, hairy leaves, and bearing dense spikes of rich pink flowers with green bracts in spring and summer.

Campanula punctata
BELLFLOWER
☼ ☼ ✳✳✳ ↕ ↔ 40cm (16in)

In early summer, this rewarding, reliable perennial produces erect stems hung with large, tubular-bell-shaped, white to dusky pink flowers, heavily spotted within.

OTHER LOW TO MEDIUM PERENNIALS FOR ALKALINE SOIL

Anthericum liliago, see p.30
Campanula glomerata 'Superba'
Centranthus ruber, see p.86
Erodium manescaui
Euphorbia rigida
Geranium sanguineum 'Max Frei', see p.76
Platycodon grandiflorus, see p.77
Scabiosa caucasica 'Clive Greaves', see p.93

Allium cristophii
ORNAMENTAL ONION
☼ ✳✳ ↕ 60cm (24in) ↔ 15cm (6in)

One of the most spectacular and reliable alliums, its large, globular heads of starry, pink-purple flowers in early summer are followed by ornamental seed heads. ♔

Delphinium tatsienense
DELPHINIUM
☼ ✳✳✳ ↕ 60cm (24in) ↔ 30cm (12in)

A refreshing change from the tall, spiked hybrids, this delightful species produces slender, branching stems of long-spurred, bright cornflower-blue flowers in summer.

Dianthus 'Mrs. Sinkins'
OLD-FASHIONED PINK
☼ ❄❄❄ ↕40cm (16in) ↔30cm (12in)

Richly fragrant of cloves, this popular
cottage-garden plant has abundant double,
fringed, white blossoms in early summer,
above evergreen, greyish green leaves.

Francoa sonchifolia
BRIDAL WREATH
☼ ◐ ❄❄ ↕90cm (36in) ↔60cm (24in)

Clumps of evergreen, deeply lobed, hairy
leaves are topped in summer by slender
pink flower sprays, marked in darker pink.
The flowers are excellent for cutting.

Geranium 'Brookside'
CRANESBILL
☼ ◐ ❄❄❄ ↕50cm (20in) ↔75cm (30in)

The finely cut leaves of this vigorous
plant form a low mound, which is covered
in summer with showers of saucer-shaped,
deep clear blue, white-eyed flowers.

Helleborus × *ericsmithii*
HELLEBORE
☼ ◐ ❄❄❄ ↕30cm (12in) ↔45cm (18in)

This bold hybrid has attractively marbled,
bristle-toothed leaves, and large, saucer-
shaped, white or pink-tinted flowers in
winter. Previously known as *H.* × *nigristern*.

Lathyrus vernus
SPRING VETCHLING
☼ ◐ ❄❄❄ ↕30cm (12in) ↔45cm (18in)

The loose racemes of purplish blue pea-
flowers in spring make this a reliable and
easily grown favourite. Its deeply divided,
glossy green leaves are attractive too. ♛

Milium effusum 'Aureum'
BOWLES' GOLDEN GRASS
☼ ❄❄❄ ↕↔60cm (24in)

Delicate in habit and golden in effect, this
is one of the brightest and most reliable of
ornamental grasses. It will seed freely and
true. Excellent for growing with *Myosotis*.

Pulsatilla vulgaris f. *alba*
PASQUE FLOWER
☼ ❄❄❄ ↕↔20cm (8in)

A beautiful white form of a popular plant,
forming a clump of finely divided, silky-
hairy leaves. Silky seed heads follow the
white spring flowers. ♛

Viola cornuta
Alba Group
HORNED VIOLET
☼ ◐ ❄❄❄ ↕15cm (6in) ↔30cm (12in)

This violet's long flowering time makes it
invaluable. A continuous supply of white
flowers tops the mat of toothy, evergreen
leaves throughout spring and summer. ♛

Medium to Tall Perennials for Alkaline Soil

NOT ALL THE PERENNIALS recommended here for alkaline soils actually prefer them to lime-free or neutral soils, but they have proved amenable to these conditions and can be relied on to do well. The following selection, around 1–3m (3–10ft) in height, represents some of the most impressive plants for these limy or chalky sites.

Euphorbia sikkimensis
SPURGE
☼ ☼ ❄❄❄ ↕ 1.2m (4ft) ↔ 60cm (24in)

The upright stems of this tough, reliable spurge bear narrow, willow-like leaves, and yellow flower clusters during summer. Bright pink new shoots appear in spring.

Cortaderia selloana 'Pumila'
PAMPAS GRASS
☼ ❄❄❄ ↕ 1.5m (5ft) ↔ 1.2m (4ft)

Although smaller than most other pampas grasses, this is an impressive specimen for a lawn. In late summer, it has crowded plumes of silvery cream spikelets. ♈

Artemisia lactiflora
WHITE MUGWORT
☼ ❄❄❄ ↕ 1.5m (5ft) ↔ 90cm (36in)

This vigorous plant has dense clumps of erect stems clothed in divided, jaggedly cut leaves. Branched heads of tiny cream flowers open in summer and autumn. ♈

Campanula lactiflora 'Loddon Anna'
BELLFLOWER
☼ ☼ ❄❄❄ ↕ 1.5m (5ft) ↔ 90cm (36in)

Reliable and easily grown, this bellflower's conical, branched heads of soft lilac-pink blooms top clumps of downy, leafy stems during summer. May need support. ♈

Eremurus robustus
DESERT CANDLE, FOXTAIL LILY
☼ ❄❄❄ ↕ 3m (10ft) ↔ 1.2m (4ft)

Magnificent, long-stemmed racemes of starry, pale pink flowers rise in summer above the clumps of strap-shaped, blue-green leaves, which wither after flowering.

Lavatera 'Barnsley'
TREE MALLOW
☼ ❄❄ ↕ ↔ 2m (6ft)

A summer-long succession of white, red-eyed flowers, and semi-evergreen, greyish green leaves, make this one of the most satisfying of all large perennials. ♈

Oenothera stricta 'Sulphurea'
EVENING PRIMROSE
☼ ❄❄❄ ↕ 90cm (36in) ↔ 15cm (6in)

Over many weeks in summer, this choice perennial bears big, fragrant, pale yellow flowers, which open in the evening on slender, erect stems. It will seed around.

Phytolacca polyandra
POKEWEED
☼ ◐ ❄❄❄ ↕ 1.2m (4ft) ↔ 60cm (24in)

A striking plant in every way. In autumn, the fleshy stems turn crimson, the leaves yellow, and dense, erect spikes of bold but poisonous, glistening black fruits appear.

Polygonatum verticillatum
WHORLED SOLOMON'S SEAL
☼ ◐ ❄❄❄ ↕ 90cm (36in) ↔ 30cm (12in)

In late spring and summer, clusters of tubular, greenish white flowers, then red berries, hang from the erect, slender stems clothed in long, narrow, willow-like leaves.

Thalictrum flavum subsp. *glaucum*
YELLOW MEADOW RUE
☼ ❄❄❄ ↕ 1.5m (5ft) ↔ 60cm (24in)

The deeply divided, blue-green, bloomy leaves of this stately plant are invaluable for contrast with greens or purples. Fluffy yellow flowerheads appear in summer. ♔

Veronicastrum virginicum f. *album*
VERONICASTRUM
☼ ◐ ❄❄❄ ↕ 2m (6ft) ↔ 60cm (24in)

Distinctive clumps of slender, stiff, erect stems, clothed in whorls of narrow, toothy leaves, carry dense, tapering spikes of white flowers from summer to autumn.

OTHER MEDIUM TO TALL PERENNIALS FOR ALKALINE SOIL

Anchusa azurea 'Loddon Royalist', see p.106
Anemone × hybrida 'Königin Charlotte', see p.50
Campanula latifolia var. *macrantha*
Centaurea macrocephala, see p.18
Cephalaria gigantea, see p.72
Lavatera 'Rosea', see p.95
Phygelius × rectus 'African Queen', see p.101

Perennials for Dry Soil in Sun

WITH THE INCREASING occurrence of droughts or water shortages in many cool-temperate regions, perennials that will tolerate dry, sunny conditions are at a premium. Fortunately, a number of plants can survive without rain or watering for long periods. Many of these have long tap-roots, or densely hairy or waxy leaf-surfaces to reduce water loss.

OTHER HERBACEOUS PERENNIALS FOR DRY SOIL IN SUN

Acanthus hirsutus, see p.20
Baptisia australis, see p.92
Cynara cardunculus, see p.130
Echinops ritro 'Veitch's Blue', see p.73
Iris 'Jane Phillips'
Linaria purpurea 'Canon J. Went'
Linum narbonense, see p.21
Oenothera stricta 'Sulphurea', see p.29
Pennisetum setaceum
Sedum 'Carmen'

Anthericum liliago
ST. BERNARD'S LILY
☼ ❄❄❄   ↕ 90cm (36in) ↔ 60cm (24in)

Popular in cottage gardens, this perennial produces elegant racemes of small, lily-like white flowers above clumps of grassy leaves in late spring and early summer. ♔

Asteriscus maritimus
ASTERICUS
☼ ❄❄   ↕ 25cm (10in) ↔ 90cm (36in)

A woody-based perennial forming a dense carpet or low mound of small, rough-hairy leaves, studded with daisy-like yellow flowerheads from late spring to summer.

Artemisia alba
ARTEMISIA
☼ ❄❄❄   ↕ 45cm (18in) ↔ 30cm (12in)

The slender, upright, grey-white stems of this dense, woody-based perennial are clothed in aromatic, filigree, silvery grey foliage, giving a plumose or frothy effect.

Catananche caerulea 'Bicolor'
BLUE CUPIDONE
☼ ❄❄❄   ↕ 50cm (20in) ↔ 30cm (12in)

This short-lived perennial forms clumps of grassy leaves. Its slender, erect stems each carry a single white, purple-centred cornflower from midsummer to autumn.

Crepis incana
PINK DANDELION
☼ ❄❄❄   ↕ ↔ 30cm (12in)

During late summer, beautiful, clear pink flowerheads, on slender-branched stems, rise over the dense grey-hairy leaf rosettes of this lovely dandelion relative. ♔

Eryngium × *tripartitum*
ERYNGIUM
☼ ❄❄❄ ↕ 60cm (24in) ↔ 50cm (20in)

Stiff, wiry, many-branched stems produce long-stalked leaves and, from summer to autumn, small heads of violet-blue flowers with prickly grey-blue bracts. ♔

Phlomis purpurea
PHLOMIS
☼ ❄❄ ↕ ↔ 60cm (24in)

A woody-based perennial or subshrub with woolly shoots and softly-hairy, grey-green leaves. In summer, clusters of pink to purple, two-lipped flowers appear.

Yucca gloriosa
SPANISH DAGGER
☼ ❄❄❄ ↕ 2m (6ft) ↔ 1m (3ft)

Evergreen, sword-shaped, spine-toothed, blue-green leaves crown the short, stout, woody stem. In late summer or autumn, a huge panicle of ivory flowers emerges. ♔

OTHER EVERGREEN PERENNIALS FOR DRY SOIL IN SUN

Achillea 'Moonshine'
Cortaderia selloana 'Pumila', see p.28
Euphorbia nicaeensis, see p.76
Iris innominata
Iris unguicularis 'Walter Butt'
Marrubium libanoticum
Phlomis russeliana
Santolina pinnata subsp. *neapolitana*
Santolina rosmarinifolia 'Primrose Gem'
Stachys byzantina 'Big Ears'

Papaver orientale 'Perry's White'
ORIENTAL POPPY
☼ ❄❄❄ ↕ ↔ 90cm (36in)

The deep-rooted clumps of stout, bristly-hairy stems, with deep-cut, rough-haired leaves, bear large, solitary white flowers with maroon-purple centres in summer.

Tropaeolum polyphyllum
TROPAEOLUM
☼ ❄❄ ↕ 10cm (4in) ↔ 1m (3ft)

Long-spurred, orange- or deep yellow blooms crowd the shoots of this vigorous, trailing plant in summer. Its lobed leaves and fleshy stems are bloomy blue-green.

Zauschneria californica subsp.
cana 'Dublin'
☼ ❄❄ ↕ 30cm (12in) ↔ 50cm (20in)

One of the best perennials for a dry site, with its low, bushy habit, narrow, downy, grey-green foliage, and tubular, bright red flowers in late summer and autumn. ♔

31

Bulbs for Dry Soil in Sun

Ａ GREAT NUMBER OF our garden bulbs, including many tulip species, foxtail lilies, and ornamental onions, come from the Mediterranean region and similar warm, sunny, dry areas of the world, including western and central Asia. None of the following bulbs enjoy shade, preferring the brightness and warmth of full sun and a site in well-drained soil. Many of these bulbs will require some protection during the winter months in cold, frost-prone regions.

Amaryllis belladonna 'Hathor'
BELLADONNA LILY
☼ ❋❋   ↕ 60cm (24in) ↔ 10cm (4in)

In time, this lily forms patches of erect, fleshy stems. These bear umbels of pure white, trumpet-shaped flowers in autumn, before the strap-shaped leaves appear.

Anemone × *fulgens*
ANEMONE
☼ ❋❋❋   ↕ 25cm (10in) ↔ 15cm (6in)

A splendid tuberous perennial, especially when planted in groups or drifts. Brilliant red flowers with darker eyes are borne in spring. It needs protection in colder areas.

Anomatheca laxa
ANOMATHECA
☼ ❋❋   ↕ 20cm (8in) ↔ 8cm (3in)

A charming little plant, free-seeding when established, especially in light or sandy soils. It has small, iris-like leaves, and bears sprays of red flowers in summer.

OTHER BULBS FOR DRY SOIL IN SUN

Allium cristophii, see p.26
Allium schubertii
Amaryllis belladonna
Anemone blanda
Anemone pavonina, see p.52
Anomatheca laxa var. *alba*
Ixiolirion tataricum
Lilium candidum
Lilium regale, see p.110
Lilium × *testaceum*
Muscari macrocarpum
Nerine bowdenii 'Mark Fenwick',
    see p.96
Ornithogalum arabicum
Oxalis adenophylla, see p.55
Pancratium illyricum, see p.41
Ranunculus asiaticus
Triteleia laxa

Arum creticum
ARUM
☼ ❋❋   ↕ 50cm (20in) ↔ 30cm (12in)

This showy plant forms healthy clumps of rich green, broadly arrow-shaped leaves. In spring, the foliage is accompanied by hooded flowers with projecting spikes.

Dracunculus vulgaris
DRAGON ARUM
☼ ❋❋   ↕ 90cm (36in) ↔ 60cm (24in)

The darkly mottled stems of this strange and striking perennial bear long-stalked, deeply divided leaves, and large, velvety, deep maroon-purple flowers in summer.

Hermodactylus tuberosus
WIDOW IRIS
☼ ✳✳✳ ↕ 30cm (12in) ↔ 10cm (4in)

This sombre but charming iris relative has narrow, grassy leaves, which are joined by green or greenish yellow flowers in spring. The outer petals have blackish brown tips.

Tulipa clusiana
LADY TULIP
☼ ✳✳✳ ↕ 30cm (12in) ↔ 10cm (4in)

A beautiful tulip of slender, elegant poise. It produces narrow grey leaves and white spring flowers with dark crimson eyes and pinkish crimson backs to the outer petals.

Eremurus stenophyllus
FOXTAIL LILY
☼ ✳✳✳ ↕ 1m (3ft) ↔ 60cm (24in)

Although not strictly a bulb, this perennial has a divided, fleshy crown that produces a cluster of strap-shaped leaves, and tall spires of starry yellow flowers in summer.

Scilla peruviana
SCILLA
☼ ✳✳ ↕ 30cm (12in) ↔ 15cm (6in)

The basal rosettes of broad, strap-shaped, fleshy green leaves are topped, during late spring, by striking, large, conical heads of small, star-shaped blue flowers.

Gladiolus communis subsp. *byzantinus*
WHISTLING JACKS
☼ ✳✳✳ ↕ 1m (3ft) ↔ 25cm (10in)

Reliable and easy to grow, this robust plant quickly forms a clump, then a patch, of leafy stems that sport bold spikes of vivid magenta flowers during summer. ♔

Triteleia hyacinthina
TRITELIA
☼ ✳✳ ↕ 70cm (28in) ↔ 5cm (2in)

Like a white-flowered ornamental onion without the smell, this very attractive and reliable bulb produces umbels of starry flowers on slender stems in early summer.

Tulipa tarda
TULIP
☼ ✳✳✳ ↕ 15cm (6in) ↔ 10cm (4in)

One of the most reliable and lovely small tulip species, producing a rosette of glossy, narrow leaves, and bearing star-shaped yellow, white-tipped flowers in spring. ♔

Perennials for Dry Soil in Shade

D RY, SHADY SITES, often found under trees and shrubs, are one of the most difficult garden situations to deal with successfully. One easy solution is to cultivate the perennials listed here, which will tolerate such conditions. If tree roots are a serious problem, the ground can also be covered with a proprietary landscaping fabric and a fresh layer of soil.

OTHER EVERGREEN PERENNIALS
FOR DRY SOIL IN SHADE

Acanthus mollis Latifolius Group
Euphorbia amygdaloides 'Purpurea'
Helleborus foetidus
Lamium galeobdolon 'Florentinum',
    see p.47
Ophiopogon japonicus
Pachyphragma macrophyllum
Reineckia carnea
Vinca major subsp. *hirsuta*, see p.51
Waldsteinia ternata

Buglossoides purpurocaerulea
PURPLE GROMWELL
☼ ◐ ❋❋❋ ↕ 60cm (24in) ↔ 90cm (36in)

This low-growing or scrambling perennial sends out long shoots that root at the tips. Erect stems bear purple flowers, turning deep blue, from late spring to summer.

Epimedium perralderianum
EPIMEDIUM
◐ ◑ ❋❋❋ ↕ 30cm (12in) ↔ 60cm (24in)

In spring, racemes of bright yellow flowers rise above the clumps of evergreen, glossy, dark green leaves, which each have three leaflets, and are bronze when young.

Claytonia sibirica
PINK PURSLANE
☼ ◑ ❋❋❋   ↕ 20cm (8in) ↔ 15cm (6in)

Short-lived but free-seeding, this plant develops tufts of fleshy green leaves and freely bears loose heads of small, pink or white flowers from late spring to summer.

Euphorbia amygdaloides var. *robbiae*
MRS. ROBB'S BONNET
☼ ◑ ❋❋❋ ↕ 75cm (30in) ↔ 60cm (24in)

A vigorous, creeping evergreen with erect stems bearing leathery, dark green leaves, and crowded racemes of greenish yellow flowers from spring to early summer. ♔

OTHER HERBACEOUS PERENNIALS
FOR DRY SOIL IN SHADE

Cyclamen hederifolium, see p.96
Dicentra eximia
Dicentra formosa
Geranium x *monacense* 'Muldoon'
Geranium nodosum
Geranium x *oxonianum* 'Claridge Druce'
Geranium phaeum 'Joan Baker'
Lunaria rediviva
Symphytum ibericum
Symphytum orientale, see p.51

Geranium phaeum 'Album'
MOURNING WIDOW
☼ ☀ ✳✳✳   ↕80cm (32in) ↔45cm (18in)

One of the loveliest geraniums, bearing showers of pendent white, yellow-beaked flowers above clumps of shallowly lobed, soft green leaves from summer to autumn.

Iris foetidissima var. *citrina*
GLADWYN
☼ ☀ ✳✳✳   ↕75cm (30in) ↔60cm (24in)

A useful and adaptable evergreen, with clumps of strong-smelling, strap-shaped, shiny leaves, and yellow summer flowers. In winter, it bears orange seed capsules.

Lamium galeobdolon 'Hermann's Pride'
☼ ☀ ✳✳✳   ↕60cm (24in) ↔1.2m (4ft)

During summer, dense mounds of erect stems bear clusters of two-lipped yellow flowers from the axils of coarsely toothed, silver-marbled, evergreen leaves.

Saxifraga stolonifera
MOTHER OF THOUSANDS
☼ ☀ ✳✳✳   ↕30cm (12in) ↔20cm (8in)

Red runners, forming new plantlets at their tips, grow from the rosettes of long-stalked, pale-veined leaves. Erect stems bear showers of white flowers in summer.

Symphytum 'Hidcote Pink'
COMFREY
☼ ☀ ✳✳✳   ↕↔45cm (18in)

Excellent for ground cover, this creeping perennial forms low patches of erect, leafy stems. Pendent clusters of funnel-shaped, pink and white flowers emerge in spring.

Tolmiea menziesii
PICK-A-BACK PLANT
☼ ☀ ✳✳✳   ↕↔60cm (24in)

A creeping perennial with loose clumps of hairy leaves that bear new plants at their bases. In spring and summer, airy panicles of tiny, brownish green flowers appear. ♔

Trachystemon orientalis
ABRAHAM-ISAAC-JACOB
☼ ☀ ✳✳✳   ↕30cm (12in) ↔indefinite

In time, this creeping plant forms large, dense patches of long-stalked, rough-hairy leaves. Its bristly stems bear blue flowers with "beaks" of stamens during spring.

Perennials for Moist Soil in Shade

OTHER PERENNIALS FOR MOIST SOIL IN SHADE

Anemonella thalictroides
Cardamine enneaphyllos
Cardamine pentaphyllos
Deinanthe bifida
Hepatica × media 'Ballardii'
Jeffersonia diphylla
Jeffersonia dubia
Mukdenia rossii
Trillium grandiflorum
Trillium grandiflorum 'Flore Pleno'

SOME OF THE MOST EXQUISITE and desirable perennials are native to deciduous woodland, where the harshness of the summer sun is filtered and weakened by branches and leaves. These woodland plants are excellent for beds on the shady side of the house and similar cool sites in the garden, where plenty of moisture is guaranteed during the growing season.

Actaea rubra
RED BANEBERRY
☀ ❄❄❄   ↕45cm (18in) ↔ 30cm (12in)

A poisonous plant, but well worth growing for its clump of deeply divided leaves, and dense, terminal clusters of shining red berries in late summer and autumn. 🏆

Convallaria majalis var. *rosea*
LILY-OF-THE-VALLEY
☀ ☀ ❄❄❄   ↕20cm (8in) ↔ 30cm (12in)

A pretty variant of a familiar and much-loved perennial, forming a carpet of paired leaves. It bears loose racemes of nodding, mauve-pink bell-flowers during spring.

Dactylorhiza foliosa
TERRESTRIAL ORCHID
☀ ❄❄❄   ↕60cm (24in) ↔ 15cm (6in)

In time, this spectacular orchid forms a clump of stout, lush, leafy stems. These sport bold, dense spikes of bright purple flowers in late spring or early summer. 🏆

Anemonopsis macrophylla
ANEMONOPSIS
☀ ❄❄❄❄ ᴾᴴ ↕75cm (30in) ↔ 45cm (18in)

This aristocrat of the woodland forms a clump of ferny leaves and bears delicate sprays of cup-shaped, nodding, waxy, lilac and violet flowers during late summer.

Corydalis flexuosa
CORYDALIS
☀ ❄❄❄   ↕↔30cm (12in)

During spring and early summer, startling showers of blue flowers rise above the ferny, blue-green foliage, which emerges in autumn and dies down in summer.

Deinanthe caerulea
DEINANTHE
☀ ❄❄❄   ↕↔30cm (12in)

The attractive, crinkly leaves of this choice, creeping perennial will eventually form a clump. Loose panicles of nodding, fleshy blue flowers open in summer.

Trillium cernuum
TRILLIUM
☼ ☼ ❄❄❄❄ PH ↕ 50cm (20in) ↔ 30cm (12in)

Impressive when planted in groups, this
charming perennial has clumps of broad,
wavy-edged leaves, and small, nodding,
white to pale pink or red flowers in spring.

Glaucidium palmatum
GLAUCIDIUM
☼ ☼ ❄❄❄ ↕↔45cm (18in)

This lovely woodlander produces a clump
of large, attractively lobed and toothed
leaves. In late spring and early summer, it
has poppy-like, mauve or lilac flowers. ♔

Trillium sessile
TOAD-SHADE
☼ ☼ ❄❄❄❄ PH ↕↔ 30cm (12in)

Quite unlike *Trillium cernuum*, and a good
contrast, this has broad, often beautifully
marbled leaves in threes, and stemless,
erect, red or maroon flowers during spring.

Hacquetia epipactis
HACQUETIA
☼ ❄❄❄ ↕ 15cm (6in) ↔ 30cm (12in)

One of the earliest woodlanders to appear
in spring, bearing curious collared, yellow-
green flowerheads, followed by emerald-
green leaves. Both useful and reliable. ♔

Sanguinaria canadensis 'Plena'
BLOODROOT
☼ ☼ ❄❄❄ ↕ 15cm (6in) ↔ 30cm (12in)

Exquisite, double white blooms open in
spring as leaves appear. The lobed, grey-
green leaves are loosely rolled around the
stems on emergence, and then unfurl. ♔

Uvularia grandiflora
LARGE MERRYBELLS
☼ ☼ ❄❄❄ ↕ 75cm (30in) ↔ 30cm (12in)

This favourite woodland plant forms a
clump of erect, slender, leafy shoots with
nodding tips. It bears pendent, tubular to
bell-shaped yellow flowers in spring. ♔

Bulbs for Moist Soil in Shade

MANY OF OUR MOST POPULAR and best-loved bulbs are found growing in the cool, moist soils and partial shade of deciduous woodlands. They include numerous snowdrops, bluebells, and erythroniums, some of which will eventually establish large colonies where space and conditions permit. Most are easy to grow in any shady, moist site.

Cardiocrinum giganteum var. *yunnanense*
GIANT LILY
☼ ❄❄❄   ↕ 2.5m (8ft) ↔ 45cm (18in)

Magnificent and monumental in flower, this perennial bears long heads of fragrant, pendent, creamy white summer blooms on tall dark stems. It dies after flowering.

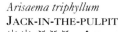

Allium moly
GOLDEN GARLIC
☼ ◑ ❄❄❄   ↕ 25cm (10in) ↔ 10cm (4in)

Quick to form substantial clumps of broad, strap-shaped grey leaves, this bulb bears umbels of starry, bright yellow flowers in early summer. Will tolerate some sun. ♈

Arisaema triphyllum
JACK-IN-THE-PULPIT
☼ ◑ ❄❄❄   ↕ 60cm (24in) ↔ 15cm (6in)

A woodland plant that will also tolerate sun. Its long-stalked green leaves, divided into threes, are accompanied in spring by hooded green, sometimes striped, flowers.

Arisaema sikokianum
ARISAEMA
☼ ❄❄   ↕ 40cm (16in) ↔ 15cm (6in)

A really striking perennial, with its leaves often beautifully marked and divided into threes. The dark flowers have contrasting white throats. Excellent grown in groups.

Brimeura amethystina
BRIMEURA
☼ ◑ ❄❄❄   ↕ 20cm (8in) ↔ 8cm (3in)

Resembling a small, slender bluebell, this bulb bears one-sided racemes of tubular, bright blue flowers in late spring or early summer. Will spread freely in a good site.

Erythronium 'Pagoda'
ERYTHRONIUM
☼ ❄❄❄   ↕ 35cm (14in) ↔ 10cm (4in)

In spring, dark stems bear pendent yellow flowers, with upswept petals, above lush rosettes of mottled green leaves. This is a vigorous bulb which soon self-seeds. ♈

OTHER BULBS FOR MOIST SOIL IN SHADE

Arisaema ringens
Arisarum proboscideum
Arum italicum 'Marmoratum', see p.135
Corydalis flexuosa 'China Blue',
    see p.65
Corydalis flexuosa 'Père David'
Cyclamen repandum
Eranthis hyemalis, see p.98
Erythronium hendersonii
Galanthus ikariae
Hyacinthoides italica
Hyacinthoides non-scripta
Ipheion uniflorum 'Froyle Mill'
Leucojum vernum
Ornithogalum nutans
Scilla bithynica
Scilla greilhuberi
Scilla liliohyacinthus

Erythronium revolutum
AMERICAN TROUT LILY
☼ ❄❄❄   ↕ 30cm (12in) ↔ 10cm (4in)

One of the best erythroniums for general cultivation, with beautifully mottled leaves, and elegant pink, yellow-centred flowers in spring. It can seed freely. ♛

Leucojum aestivum 'Gravetye Giant'
SUMMER SNOWFLAKE
☼ ☼ ❄❄❄   ↕ 90cm (36in) ↔ 10cm (4in)

Erect clumps of green leaves are quickly formed by this robust, easily grown bulb. The umbels of nodding white, green-tipped flowers emerge in late spring. ♛

Galanthus elwesii
GIANT SNOWDROP
☼ ❄❄❄   ↕ 22cm (9in) ↔ 8cm (3in)

Easy to grow and reliable, this variable bulb usually has narrow, grey-green leaves, and white flowers in late winter, the inner segments marked green at both ends. ♛

Galanthus plicatus
SNOWDROP
☼ ❄❄❄   ↕ 20cm (8in) ↔ 8cm (3in)

In time, this vigorous snowdrop will form colonies. Its blue-green leaves have edges folded under, and its late winter flowers have green-tipped inner segments. ♛

Narcissus pseudonarcissus
LENT LILY
☼ ☼ ❄❄❄   ↕ 35cm (14in) ↔ 10cm (4in)

A charming woodland species, and parent of many hybrids. Its pale yellow spring flowers have deep yellow trumpets, flared at the mouths. Excellent for naturalizing.

Perennials for Warm, Sheltered Sites

OR THOSE FORTUNATE ENOUGH to garden in mild areas, there are many exciting, often exotic-looking perennials that can be grown with little effort. Some of these will also survive in colder areas in a warm, sheltered site, especially in cities where favourable microclimates often occur. They can also be grown in containers and moved indoors for winter.

Erythrina crista-galli
COCK'S COMB
☼ ❋❋   ↕ 2m (6ft) ↔ 1.2m (4ft)

Herbaceous or woody-based in cold areas, this perennial forms a shrub or small tree in frost-free regions. Strong, thorny stems bear red pea-flowers in late summer. ♛

Begonia sutherlandii
TUBEROUS BEGONIA
☼ ❋   ↕↔ 45cm (18in)

In summer, low hummocks of fleshy red stems, with long-pointed, toothed leaves, freely bear drooping clusters of orange, red-stalked flowers. ♛

Bletilla striata 'Albostriata'
BLETILLA
☼ ☼ ❋   ↕↔ 60cm (24in)

A beautiful ground orchid, eventually forming patches of strongly veined, white-margined, bamboo-like leaves. Magenta flowers open in spring and early summer.

Crinum × *powellii*
CRINUM
☼ ❋❋   ↕ 1.2m (4ft) ↔ 60cm (24in)

Stout, fleshy stems carry loose umbels of fragrant, lily-like pink blooms above the bold clumps of long, arching, strap-shaped leaves from late summer to autumn. ♛

Eucomis comosa
PINEAPPLE FLOWER
☼ ❋❋   ↕ 60cm (24in) ↔ 30cm (12in)

Dense racemes of greenish white flowers, with leafy tufts at the top, rise on fleshy stems during late summer, above rosettes of strap-shaped, shiny green leaves.

Fascicularia pitcairniifolia
FASCICULARIA
☼ ❄   ↕ ↔ 60cm (24in)

A striking relative of the pineapple, with narrow, spine-toothed, evergreen leaves in bold rosettes. In summer, the inner leaves turn red when powdery blue flowers open.

OTHER HERBACEOUS PERENNIALS FOR WARM, SHELTERED SITES

Begonia grandis subsp. *evansiana*
Canna iridiflora
Commelina coelestis
Eucomis bicolor, see p.64
Gladiolus callianthus
Gladiolus cardinalis
Impatiens tinctoria
Leonotis ocymifolia
Lobelia tupa
Musa basjoo

Lobelia laxiflora var. *angustifolia*
LOBELIA
☼ ❄❄❄   ↕ 60cm (24in) ↔ 1m (3ft)

The erect, woody-based stems of this fast-spreading lobelia bear narrow, willow-like leaves, and lax, tubular, red and yellow flowers in late spring and early summer.

Melianthus major
HONEY BUSH
☼ ❄   ↕ 2m (6ft) ↔ 1m (3ft)

A spectacular foliage plant with a clump of hollow stems, large, lush, sharp-toothed and deeply divided, blue-grey leaves, and spikes of brownish red flowers in summer.

Puya alpestris
PUYA
☼ ❄❄❄   ↕ 1.5m (5ft) ↔ 1.4m (4½ft)

After several years, the evergreen rosette of narrow, spine-toothed leaves produces an erect stem topped by a striking, dense spike of waxy, blue-green summer blooms.

OTHER EVERGREEN PERENNIALS FOR WARM, SHELTERED SITES

Agapanthus praecox subsp. *orientalis*
Astelia chathamica
Beschorneria yuccoides
Dicksonia antarctica, see p.122
Eryngium proteiflorum
Fascicularia bicolor
Geranium maderense
Myosotidium hortensia
Puya chilensis, see p.120
Wachendorfia thyrsiflora

Hedychium gardnerianum
GINGER LILY
☼ ❄❄❄   ↕ 2m (6ft) ↔ 1m (3ft)

This vigorous perennial forms a clump of erect, leafy stems that bear large heads of fragrant, pale yellow flowers, with long, red stamens, during late summer.

Pancratium illyricum
SEA LILY
☼ ❄   ↕ ↔ 40cm (16in)

In late summer, this bulbous perennial produces umbels of fragrant, star-shaped white flowers on erect stems above a clump of strap-shaped, grey-green leaves.

Senecio pulcher
SENECIO
☼ ❄❄❄   ↕ 60cm (24in) ↔ 50cm (20in)

The basal clumps of semi-evergreen, long, scalloped leaves are woolly when young. Attractive, large, carmine-purple, yellow-centred flowerheads emerge in summer.

SPECIFIC USES

WHETHER YOU WANT plants to fill a difficult site, to provide cut flowers or foliage, or to attract bees and butterflies to your garden, perennials have the variety and versatility to answer your needs. A good choice of plants is usually available to solve even the most specific garden problems.

Houttuynia cordata 'Chameleon' for water gardens

△ LOVED BY BUTTERFLIES *The flowers of perennials like* Inula hookeri *attract bees, butterflies, and other welcome insects.*

The plants in this section have been selected to help you find the right perennials for specific garden features (such as rock or water gardens), conditions (including dry, exposed, or waterlogged sites), and garden problems (like pollution or pests). When choosing plants for a particular garden feature or site, the most suitable are usually those that grow in similar situations in the wild. Water and bog gardens, for instance, require plants that are naturally tolerant of wet soils. At the other extreme, rock gardens and screes are suited to perennials that thrive, if not depend, on sharp drainage. Similarly, coastal gardens in exposed sites require robust perennials like eryngiums that are adapted to the harsh conditions. Toughness and persistence are also needed by plants naturalized in grass, hedge bottoms, or other wild areas, where the ability to withstand competition is vital for survival.

PROBLEM SOLVERS
Perennials offer more than just a wide range of options for specific sites; they can also help us address some of the problems that often plague our gardens. Pests, such as snails, deer, and rabbits, may be thwarted by a surprising number of unpalatable plants. The garden can also be stocked with many low-allergen (mostly insect-pollinated) perennials, useful for gardeners who suffer from allergies that are aggravated or induced by plants.

DECORATIVE USES
The wide-ranging ornamental value of perennials is not always fully appreciated. Many are ideal for containers on a shady or sunny patio or paved area, or for specimen plants. Others have foliage and flowers good for cutting, extending their garden value into the home. During quiet periods in the garden, dried seed heads can provide the material for arrangements.

△ NATURAL EFFECT *Many perennials, especially bulbs like these fritillaries, are excellent for naturalizing in grassy sites.*

◁ ROCK GARDEN *Perennials from well-drained, rocky habitats in the wild will thrive in a rock garden, wall, or scree bed.*

▷ WATERSIDE *A pond planted with lush marginal and aquatic perennials makes a bold feature and a good wildlife habitat.*

Perennials for Ground Cover in Sun

GROUND COVER PLANTS, while ornamental, also perform one of the most useful and valuable jobs in the garden by clothing bare ground. They are usually fast-growing, and the following, given a sunny site, will repay your confidence in them by providing a superb display of foliage and flowers. For even faster results, plant these perennials in groups.

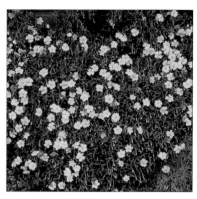

Helianthemum lunulatum
ROCK ROSE, SUN ROSE
☼ ✳✳✳ ↕ 15cm (6in) ↔ 30cm (12in)

A carpeting, woody-based perennial with evergreen, hairy, greyish green leaves, and clusters of yellow flowers with orange-yellow stamens in late spring and summer.

OTHER EVERGREEN PERENNIALS FOR GROUND COVER IN SUN

Acaena 'Blue Haze'
Arabis x *arendsii* 'Rosabella'
Aubrieta 'Joy'
Cerastium tomentosum, see p.130
Geranium sanguineum var. *striatum*
Globularia cordifolia
Helianthemum 'Rhodanthe Carneum'
Lamium maculatum f. *album*
Persicaria affinis 'Donald Lowndes'
Veronica peduncularis 'Georgia Blue'

Ceratostigma plumbaginoides
HARDY PLUMBAGO
☼ ✳✳✳ ↕ 30cm (12in) ↔ 45cm (18in)

This creeping perennial eventually forms a dense patch of leafy reddish stems that turn red-orange in autumn. Clusters of rich blue flowers open in late summer. ♈

Diascia 'Salmon Supreme'
DIASCIA
☼ ✳✳✳ ↕ 15cm (6in) ↔ 50cm (20in)

Free-flowering over a long period during summer and autumn, the slender racemes of pale flowers rise above semi-evergreen mats of small, heart-shaped leaves.

Geranium 'Ann Folkard'
CRANESBILL
☼ ☼ ✳✳✳ ↕ 60cm (24in) ↔ 1.5m (5ft)

Few cranesbills will flower or scramble as freely as this one, with its dense blanket of deeply lobed, yellow-green leaves, and magenta flowers in summer and autumn.

Persicaria vacciniifolia
PERSICARIA
☼ ☼ ✳✳✳ ↕ 15cm (6in) ↔ 30cm (12in)

This fast-creeping plant forms a carpet of small, glossy leaves that colour richly in autumn. Its erect, deep pink flower spikes open from late summer into autumn. ♈

OTHER HERBACEOUS PERENNIALS FOR GROUND COVER IN SUN

Alchemilla alpina
Gunnera magellanica
Hippocrepis comosa
Hypsella reniformis
Oenothera macrocarpa, see p.101
Phuopsis stylosa
Potentilla aurea
Saponaria ocymoides
Scutellaria orientalis
Tropaeolum polyphyllum, see p.31

Phyla nodiflora
CAPEWEED, MATGRASS
☼ ✳✳✳   ↕5cm (2in) ↔ indefinite

Sometimes sold as *Lippia*, this perennial soons forms carpets of slender stems and small leaves. Its long-stalked clusters of tiny flowers open in summer and autumn.

Silene schafta
CAMPION
☼ ◐ ✳✳✳   ↕25cm (10in) ↔ 30cm (12in)

Slender stems and semi-evergreen, bright green leaves form a low mound, good for edging. Long-tubed, red-pink flowers are borne freely from summer to autumn. ♈

Rhodanthemum hosmariense
RHODANTHEMUM
☼ ✳✳   ↕↔30cm (12in)

A low and spreading, woody-based plant with dense, finely divided, silvery downy leaves. The large daisy-flowers are borne freely from early spring to autumn. ♈

Sedum spurium 'Schorbuser Blut'
STONECROP
☼ ✳✳✳   ↕10cm (4in) ↔ 60cm (24in)

Popular as a vigorous carpeter, this stone-crop has glossy, evergreen leaves that are purple-tinted when mature. Starry, deep pink flowers open in late summer. ♈

Stachys byzantina
LAMB'S EARS
☼ ✳✳✳   ↕38cm (15in) ↔ 60cm (24in)

The white-woolly leaves and prostrate stems provide effective, evergreen ground cover. White-woolly, pink-purple flower spikes rise above the foliage in summer.

Perennials for Ground Cover in Shade

SHADY AREAS CAN SUPPORT a wealth of plants, as long as the soil remains sufficiently moist. A number of shade-loving perennials are naturally creeping or otherwise spreading and low-growing, and are useful and attractive as ground cover beneath shrubs or trees. Many are also evergreen, and will brighten shady spots with their year-round carpets of foliage.

Cyclamen repandum subsp. *peloponnesiacum*

☼ ☀ ❄❄❄❄   ‡ 10cm (4in) ↔ 15cm (6in)

A tuberous perennial that forms patches of scalloped, heart-shaped, silver-speckled leaves. In spring, it bears fragrant, pale pink flowers with dark mouths. ♈

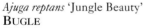

Ajuga reptans 'Jungle Beauty'
BUGLE
☼ ☀ ❄❄❄❄   ‡ 15cm (6in) ↔ 1m (3ft)

Grown here with *Lysimachia nummularia* 'Aurea', this semi-evergreen, far-creeping carpeter has shiny, bronze-green leaves, and rich blue flower spikes in late spring.

OTHER EVERGREEN PERENNIALS FOR GROUND COVER IN SHADE

Blechnum penna-marina
Cardamine trifolia
Euphorbia amygdaloides var. *robbiae*, see p.34
Saxifraga rotundifolia
Saxifraga spathularis
Saxifraga × geum 'Dentata'
Symphytum ibericum
Tiarella wherryi
Waldsteinia ternata

Duchesnea indica
INDIAN STRAWBERRY
☼ ☀ ❄❄❄❄   ‡ 10cm (4in) ↔ 1.2m (4ft)

The dense, fast-growing, evergreen carpet of strawberry-like leaves is peppered with yellow flowers in summer. The fruits resemble strawberries but are unpalatable.

Chrysogonum virginianum
CHRYSOGONUM   ☼ ☀ ☀
❄❄❄   ‡ 25cm (10in) ↔ 60cm (24in)

This fast-growing woodland plant forms dense carpets of small, semi-evergreen leaves. Bright and cheerful yellow flowers are produced during spring and summer.

Epimedium pinnatum subsp. *colchicum*
EPIMEDIUM
☼ ☀ ❄❄❄❄   ‡ ↔ 40cm (16in)

One of the most reliable epimediums, with clumps of evergreen, softly prickle-margined leaves, topped by loose spires of four-petalled yellow flowers in spring. ♈

Tiarella cordifolia
FOAM FLOWER
☼ ☀ ❄❄❄ ↕ 25cm (10in) ↔ 30cm (12in)

A reliable old favourite, especially pretty
in late spring, when foamy spires of white
flowers rise above the evergreen foliage.
The leaves are often tinted in autumn. ♔

Geranium macrorrhizum 'Czakor'
CRANESBILL
☼ ☀ ❄❄❄ ↕ 30cm (12in) ↔ 60cm (24in)

A first-rate carpeter, with prettily lobed,
aromatic, evergreen leaves, which become
purple-tinted in autumn. It bears profuse,
small magenta flowers in early summer.

Lamium galeobdolon 'Florentinum'
YELLOW ARCHANGEL
☼ ☀ ❄❄❄ ↕ 60cm (24in) ↔ 2m (6ft)

One of the most striking, but invasive,
ground-cover perennials. It has evergreen,
silver-zoned leaves, and bears spires of
two-lipped yellow flowers in summer.

Gymnocarpium dryopteris
OAK FERN
☼ ☀ ❄❄❄ [PH] ↕ 20cm (8in) ↔ 30cm (12in)

Delicate looking but hardy, this little fern
forms a low patch of triangular, prettily
divided fronds on slender, wiry stems.
The fronds turn rich green with age. ♔

Meehania urticifolia
MEEHANIA
☼ ☀ ❄❄❄ ↕ 30cm (12in) ↔ 2m (6ft)

In time, this vigorous perennial forms
clumps of heart-shaped leaves. One-sided
spikes of two-lipped, deep violet flowers
are borne in late spring and early summer.

Vinca minor 'Gertrude Jekyll'
LESSER PERIWINKLE
☼ ☀ ❄❄❄ ↕ 15cm (6in) ↔ indefinite

Strictly a creeping shrub, but excellent
ground cover for use with perennials. The
pure white flowers in spring and summer
contrast with the dark green leaves. ♔

**OTHER HERBACEOUS PERENNIALS
FOR GROUND COVER IN SHADE**

Adiantum pedatum, see p.119
Aegopodium podagraria 'Variegatum'
Anemone nemorosa 'Flore Pleno'
Anemone nemorosa 'Robinsoniana'
Arisarum proboscideum
Convallaria majalis 'Fortin's Giant'
Cyclamen hederifolium, see p.96
Galium odoratum
Maianthemum bifolium
Trachystemon orientalis, see p.35

Perennial Herbs for Borders

PERENNIALS VALUED FOR either their culinary or medicinal attributes are frequently cultivated together in herb or kitchen gardens, or borders and beds. This certainly makes it much more convenient for picking or harvesting, but does not always make the best use of these plants' varied growth habits, or their often ornamental foliage and flowers. In fact, they can be grown just as easily, and more effectively, with other perennials in mixed plantings in the garden.

Achillea ptarmica 'Boule de Neige'
SNEEZEWORT
☀ ❄❄❄ ↕ 60cm (24in) ↔ 45cm (18in)

During summer, the clump of erect stems, with narrow, toothed, dark green leaves, is smothered in small, double white flower-heads. All parts have medicinal uses.

Allium schoenoprasum 'Forescate'
CHIVES
☀ ❄❄❄ ↕ 60cm (24in) ↔ 12.5cm (5in)

An attractive, vigorous form of a kitchen-garden favourite, with clumps of edible, hollow leaves, and dense heads of bright purplish pink flowers in summer.

Aristolochia clematitis
BIRTHWORT
☀ ☀ ❄❄❄ ↕ 90cm (36in) ↔ 60cm (24in)

Curious, slender-tubed yellow flowers emerge from the axils of the heart-shaped leaves in summer. The creeping rootstock forms clumps and patches of erect stems.

Agastache foeniculum
ANISE HYSSOP
☀ ❄❄❄ ↕ 90cm (36in) ↔ 45cm (18in)

Spikes of blue flowers with violet bracts top the four-angled stems in summer. The softly-downy, aniseed-scented leaves are used as a fragrant tea and in pot-pourri.

Althaea officinalis
MARSH MALLOW
☀ ☀ ❄❄❄ ↕ 2m (6ft) ↔ 1.5m (5ft)

Loose clumps of downy stems bear three-lobed, velvety, greyish leaves, and white or pale pink late-summer flowers. Its root sugars were once used for marshmallow.

OTHER PERENNIAL HERBS FOR BORDERS

Armoracia rusticana 'Variegata', see p.126
Cichorium intybus 'Roseum', see p.76
Foeniculum vulgare 'Purpureum', see p.119
Melittis melissophyllum, see p.73
Mentha suaveolens 'Variegata'
Meum athamanticum, see p.119
Monarda fistulosa
Origanum vulgare 'Gold Tip'
Persicaria bistorta
Pulmonaria officinalis
Salvia officinalis 'Icterina', see p.121
Saponaria officinalis 'Rosea Plena'
Scutellaria baicalensis
Symphytum peregrinum 'Rubrum'
Tanacetum balsamita subsp. *balsamitoides*

Melissa officinalis 'Aurea'
LEMON BALM
☼ ❄❄❄ ↕60cm (24in) ↔45cm (18in)

The hairy green, yellow-splashed leaves
of this vigorous, bushy plant are lemon-
scented when bruised. The tiny flowers,
loved by bees, are borne in summer.

Myrrhis odorata
SWEET CICELY, WILD ANISEED
☼ ◐ ❄❄❄ ↕90cm (36in) ↔1.5m (5ft)

All parts of this plant are aniseed-scented.
It has bold clumps of hollow stems, large,
ferny leaves, and flattened heads of white
summer flowers, followed by brown fruits.

Rumex scutatus 'Silver Shield'
FRENCH SORREL
☼ ❄❄❄ ↕50cm (20in) ↔30cm (12in)

This small, woody-based perennial has
prostrate and upright stems with broadly
arrow-shaped, silver-green-topped leaves.
Spires of green flowers open in summer.

Levisticum officinale
LOVAGE
☼ ❄❄❄ ↕2m (6ft) ↔1m (3ft)

Much-divided, dark green leaves clothe
the bold, erect clumps of smooth, hollow
stems. These are topped by umbels of
greenish yellow flowers during summer.

Origanum vulgare 'Aureum'
GOLDEN WILD MARJORAM
☼ ❄❄❄ ↕45cm (18in) ↔30cm (12in)

The dense clumps of four-angled stems,
crowded with rounded, aromatic golden
leaves, bear dense clusters of pink flowers
from summer into autumn. ♔

Salvia officinalis 'Tricolor'
COMMON SAGE
☼ ❄❄❄ ↕80cm (32in) ↔1m (3ft)

A woody-based, evergreen perennial or
bushy subshrub, bearing aromatic, woolly,
grey-green leaves with cream, purple, and
pink zones. It has blue flowers in summer.

49

Perennials for Hedge Bottoms and Wild Margins

MANY OF THE LOVELIEST WILD FLOWERS are frequently found thriving beside roads or at the bases of hedges. They provide some of the most colourful displays in rural areas, and there is no reason why similar effects should not be created within our gardens, making use of perennials that can tolerate competition from other plants in the same way.

SPECIFIC USES

Heliopsis helianthoides subsp. *scabra* 'Sommersonne'

☼ ❄❄❄   ↕ 90cm (36in) ↔ 60cm (24in)

The bold clumps of leafy, branched stems carry large, single to semi-double, golden yellow daisy-heads, with brownish yellow centres, from late summer to autumn.

Anemone x *hybrida* 'Königin Charlotte'
JAPANESE ANEMONE

☼ ☼ ❄❄❄   ↕ 1.5m (5ft) ↔ indefinite

A vigorous perennial forming colonies of branched stems with handsome, downy, grey-green leaves. Big, semi-double pink flowers open in late summer and autumn.

Carex pendula
PENDULOUS SEDGE

☼ ☼ ❄❄❄   ↕ 1.2m (4ft) ↔ 1.5m (5ft)

Arching, three-cornered stems and dark green leaves form large clumps, topped in late spring and summer by long, pendent green flower spikes. Prefers moist shade.

Lathyrus latifolius
PERENNIAL PEA

☼ ❄❄❄   ↕ ↔ 2m (6ft)

From summer to autumn, this vigorous, herbaceous climber produces long-stalked racemes of pink or purple pea-flowers on long, scrambling, winged stems.   ⚜

Campanula latifolia
GIANT BELLFLOWER

☼ ☼ ❄❄❄   ↕ 1.5m (5ft) ↔ 60cm (24in)

In summer, the stout clumps of vigorous, erect, leafy stems produce large, tubular, pale to deep violet or white bell-flowers from the axils of the uppermost leaves.

Helianthus x *multiflorus*
PERENNIAL SUNFLOWER

☼ ❄❄❄   ↕ 2m (6ft) ↔ 90cm (36in)

Dark green leaves clothe the tall clumps of branching stems, which produce yellow, dark-centred daisy-heads in late summer and autumn. It prefers a moist site.

OTHER EVERGREEN PERENNIALS FOR WILD AREAS

Epimedium x *perralchicum*
Epimedium pinnatum subsp. *colchicum*, see p.46
Euphorbia amygdaloides var. *robbiae*, see p.34
Iris foetidissima var. *citrina*, see p.35
Lamium galeobdolon 'Florentinum', see p.47
Luzula sylvatica
Polystichum setiferum, see p.140

Lysimachia punctata
LOOSESTRIFE
☼ ☼ ❄❄❄   ↕ 1m (3ft) ↔ 60cm (24in)

A reliable, robust perennial with clumps of leafy, erect stems. In summer, the leaf axils are crowded with cup-shaped yellow flowers. Too invasive for beds or borders.

OTHER HERBACEOUS PERENNIALS FOR WILD AREAS
Campanula rapunculoides
Campanula trachelium
Cicerbita plumieri
Dryopteris filix-mas
Leucanthemum × *superbum*
Myrrhis odorata, see p.49
Pentaglottis sempervirens, see p.75
Persicaria amplexicaulis
Salvia glutinosa
Symphytum caucasicum

Saponaria officinalis 'Rubra Plena'
SOAPWORT
☼ ❄❄❄   ↕ ↔ 90cm (36in)

The creeping rootstock of this reliable, easily grown plant forms patches of leafy stems, crowned in summer with clusters of fragrant, double, rose-pink flowers.

Rumex sanguineus
BLOODY DOCK
☼ ❄❄❄   ↕ 90cm (36in) ↔ 30cm (12in)

This tap-rooted dock is valued mainly for its rosetted, red- or purple-veined leaves. In autumn, erect stems first bear clusters of tiny green flowers, then brown fruits.

Symphytum orientale
WHITE COMFREY   ☼ ☼ ☀
❄❄❄   ↕ 70cm (28in) ↔ 45cm (18in)

Nodding clusters of funnel-shaped white flowers open on the erect, little-branched stems of this hairy plant in late spring and early summer. It tolerates dry shade. ♔

Vinca major subsp. *hirsuta*
GREATER PERIWINKLE
☼ ☼ ❄❄❄❄   ↕ 45cm (18in) ↔ indefinite

This vigorous, scrambling or creeping, evergreen perennial or subshrub produces narrow-lobed violet flowers as new shoots emerge in spring, and into summer.

Bulbs for Naturalizing

THERE ARE FEW SIGHTS in the plant world more inspiring than a meadow, woodland floor, or alpine pasture studded with wild flowers, creating a carpet of colour as far as the eye can see. Bulbs especially lend themselves to such displays and, where space permits in the garden, there is a multitude of species and varieties that can be used for this purpose. For a natural effect, plant bulbs in scattered groups, with space between to allow for expansion or self-seeding.

Erythronium dens-canis
DOG'S-TOOTH VIOLET
☼ ☀ ❄❄❄   ↕15cm (6in) ↔ 10cm (4in)

The exquisite, pinkish purple flowers are poised above rosettes of fleshy, beautifully mottled leaves in spring. Excellent for use in short grass and in woodland. ♛

Anemone pavonina
ANEMONE
☼ ❄❄❄   ↕25cm (10in) ↔ 15cm (6in)

This feathery-leaved anemone is ideal for sunny, well-drained sites in short grass or borders. Glowing red flowers with a white ring and dark eye are spectacular in spring.

Crocus vernus 'Jeanne d'Arc'
DUTCH CROCUS
☼ ❄❄❄   ↕12cm (5in) ↔ 5cm (2in)

Attractive and reliable, this large-flowered crocus soon forms clumps or patches in short grass or borders. White flowers with orange stigmas are produced in spring.

Fritillaria meleagris
SNAKE'S HEAD FRITILLARY
☼ ☀ ❄❄❄   ↕30cm (12in) ↔ 8cm (3in)

A uniquely charming bulb, with narrow, greyish leaves, and nodding, chequered bell-flowers on slender stems in spring. It thrives in moist grass or beneath shrubs.

Camassia leichtlinii
CAMASSIA
☼ ☀ ❄❄   ↕1.3m (4½ft) ↔ 10cm (4in)

An easily grown bulb, suitable for moist meadows or grassy sites. Long spires of star-shaped, blue or white flowers rise in summer above the slender leaves. ♛

OTHER BULBS FOR NATURALIZING IN SHADE

Anemone blanda 'Atrocaerulea'
Arisarum proboscideum
Arum italicum 'Marmoratum', see p.135
Colchicum speciosum
Crocus kotschyanus
Crocus tommasinianus, see p.98
Cyclamen coum
Cyclamen hederifolium, see p.96
Cyclamen repandum
Eranthis hyemalis, see p.98
Erythronium oregonum
Galanthus elwesii, see p.39
Hyacinthoides non-scripta
Lilium pyrenaicum
Narcissus 'Golden Harvest'
Narcissus 'Mount Hood', see p.85
Ornithogalum nutans
Scilla bithynica

Galanthus nivalis
COMMON SNOWDROP
☼ ❄❄❄   ↕↔ 10cm (4in)

Large drifts of this familiar woodland snowdrop are spectacular in early spring. It naturalizes readily by seed and division, and will tolerate sun if the soil is moist. ♛

Nectaroscordum siculum
NECTAROSCORDUM
☼ ☀ ❄❄❄❄   ↕ 1.2m (4ft) ↔ 10cm (4in)

In summer, tall, strong stems sport loose
umbels of drooping green bell-flowers,
flushed with purple. The straw-coloured
seed capsules are equally ornamental.

Hyacinthoides hispanica of gardens
SPANISH BLUEBELL
☼ ☀ ❄❄❄   ↕ 40cm (16in) ↔ 10cm (4in)

This robust bulb forms large patches of
shiny green leaves, with nodding blue
flowers borne on strong stems in spring.
It may be too vigorous for a small garden.

Tulipa sylvestris
TULIP
☼ ❄❄❄   ↕ 45cm (18in) ↔ 10cm (4in)

This tulip is easily established in grass-
land or in open woodland, where it forms
patches. Star-shaped yellow flowers open
in spring, but are not always freely borne.

Lilium martagon
MARTAGON LILY
☼ ☀ ❄❄❄   ↕ 2m (6ft) ↔ 25cm (10in)

An old and reliable lily for naturalizing in
grass or in a border. The tall stems bear
whorled leaves, and panicles of nodding
flowers in a variety of colours in summer.

Narcissus bulbocodium
HOOP-PETTICOAT DAFFODIL
☼ ❄❄❄   ↕ 15cm (6in) ↔ 8cm (3in)

A real charmer with its narrow, thread-like
leaves, and striking, funnel-shaped, pale
yellow flowers in spring. It will thrive and
seed itself on a moist, grassy, sloping site.

**OTHER BULBS FOR NATURALIZING
IN SUN**

Allium flavum
Allium unifolium
Anemone coronaria
Camassia quamash
Chionodoxa luciliae, see p.90
Colchicum autumnale
Gladiolus communis subsp. *byzantinus*,
  see p.33
Gladiolus papilio
Lilium duchartrei
Lilium hansonii
Lilium pardalinum
Narcissus obvallaris
Nectaroscordum siculum subsp.
  bulgaricum
Tulipa kaufmanniana
Zantedeschia aethiopica 'Crowborough',
  see p.61

Perennials for Rock Gardens and Screes

SOME OF THE LOVELIEST and most satisfying flowering perennials are those suitable for growing on rock gardens and screes. Many of these plants have a carpeting habit and will provide excellent ground cover in the garden. Others form small clumps or low hummocks, and associate well with miniature bulbs, such as chionodoxas, crocuses, and scillas.

Dianthus 'Pike's Pink'
ALPINE PINK
☼ ❄❄❄   ↕15cm (6in) ↔ 20cm (8in)

The low, evergreen cushion of narrow, blue-grey leaves is topped in summer by double pale pink flowers, darker zoned in cerise, and with a delicious clove scent. ♔

OTHER PERENNIALS FOR ROCK GARDENS AND SCREES

Anthemis marschalliana
Armeria juniperifolia
Euphorbia myrsinites
Gentiana acaulis
Geranium argenteum
Hypericum olympicum 'Sulphureum'
Iris pumila
Linaria alpina
Phlox subulata 'Amazing Grace'
Potentilla nitida

Aethionema 'Warley Rose'
STONE CRESS
☼ ❄❄❄   ↕ ↔ 20cm (8in)

A long-established favourite, forming an evergreen hummock of slender stems with narrow, blue-grey leaves. Its pink flowers open in late spring and early summer. ♔

Anthyllis montana
ANTHYLLIS
☼ ❄❄❄   ↕30cm (12in) ↔ 60cm (24in)

In summer, the dense carpet of deeply divided, silky, grey-green leaves is covered with rounded, clover-like heads of pink to purple, white-tipped flowers.

Diascia 'Blackthorn Apricot'
DIASCIA
☼ ❄❄   ↕25cm (10in) ↔ 50cm (20in)

This is a gem among the numerous new diascias. In summer, it bears abundant, slender racemes of apricot flowers above the mat or carpet of trailing green stems.

Anemone sylvestris
SNOWDROP ANEMONE
☼ ◑ ❄❄❄   ↕ ↔ 30cm (12in)

This low-grower forms patches of deeply cut, ferny leaves. Pure white flowers with gold stamens appear in spring and early summer, followed by silky seed heads.

Campanula carpatica 'Chewton Joy'
BELLFLOWER
☼ ◑ ❄❄❄ ↕30cm (12in) ↔ 50cm (20in)

The low, trailing stems are clothed with toothed, heart-shaped leaves, and bear upturned blue bell-flowers with paler centres over several months in summer.

OTHER PERENNIALS FOR ROCK
GARDENS WITH LIME-FREE SOIL

Celmisia spectabilis
Dodecatheon meadia f. *album*, see p.24
Houstonia michauxii
Lewisia Cotyledon Hybrids, see p.59
Lithodora diffusa 'Heavenly Blue'
Oxalis enneaphylla
Phlox adsurgens 'Wagon Wheel'
Phlox × *procumbens* 'Millstream'
Potentilla aurea
Tanakaea radicans

Gentiana sino-ornata
AUTUMN GENTIAN
☀ ◐ ❄❄❄❄ ᴾᴴ ↕ 7cm (3in) ↔ 30cm (12in)

One of the most famous and spectacular
autumn-flowering gentians, with an overwintering mat of trailing, leafy stems and
upturned, deep blue trumpet flowers. ♛

Gypsophila repens 'Rosa Schönheit'
ALPINE GYPSOPHILA
☀ ❄❄❄ ↕ 20cm (8in) ↔ 50cm (20in)

Also known as 'Pink Beauty', as the semi-
evergreen mat of slender, bluish green
stems and leaves is smothered for many
weeks in summer by tiny pink flowers.

Geranium cinereum 'Ballerina'
CRANESBILL
☀ ◐ ❄❄❄ ↕ 15cm (6in) ↔ 30cm (12in)

A neat little perennial, producing a loose
hummock of small, grey-green leaves, and
purplish red flowers with dark veins and
eyes over a long period in summer. ♛

Oxalis adenophylla
ALPINE OXALIS
☀ ❄❄❄ ↕ 10cm (4in) ↔ 15cm (6in)

The tuft of deeply divided, greyish green
leaves is accompanied during spring by
funnel-shaped, purplish pink flowers with
pale centres and dark throats. ♛

Roscoea cautleoides 'Kew Beauty'
ROSCOEA
☀ ◐ ❄❄❄ ↕ 40cm (16in) ↔ 15cm (6in)

Appearing in late spring, this gorgeous
perennial produces a small clump of erect,
leafy stems, which bear loose spikes of
large, pale yellow, orchid-like flowers.

Bulbs for Rock Gardens and Screes

ROCK GARDENS, RAISED BEDS, AND SCREES are ideal sites for cultivating the many miniature bulbs available for the garden, as well as for larger bulbous plants, such as *Eucomis*, which like well-drained, gritty soil and full sun. Most of the following are hardy, and should be planted in groups or drifts for best effect. They are also suitable for containers.

Eucomis autumnalis
EUCOMIS
☀ ❋❋❋ ↕ 30cm (12in) ↔ 20cm (8in)

Fleshy stems bear crowded, green-white flower spikes in late summer and autumn, above bold clumps of broad, strap-shaped, wavy-edged leaves. Likes a sheltered site.

Allium narcissiflorum
ORNAMENTAL ONION
☀ ❋❋❋ ↕ 30cm (12in) ↔ 5cm (2in)

This choice species forms a small clump of grass-like, grey-green leaves. Clusters of nodding, red-purple or pale pink bell-flowers open on upright stems in summer.

Colchicum kesselringii
COLCHICUM
☀ ❋❋❋ ↕ ↔ 3cm (1¼in)

Ideal for a sheltered, well-drained pocket, this lovely bulb has white flowers – like miniature crocuses – in late winter and spring. The petal backs are purple-striped.

Fritillaria pallidiflora
FRITILLARIA
☀ ❋❋❋ ↕ 40cm (16in) ↔ 7.5cm (3in)

During late spring and early summer, this handsome bulb bears nodding, creamy yellow bell-flowers from the axils of long, narrow, bloomy grey-green leaves. ▽

Chionodoxa forbesii
SNOW GLORY
☀ ❋❋❋ ↕ 20cm (8in) ↔ 10cm (4in)

A free-flowering, reliable bulb, forming small tufts of narrow green leaves. In early spring, it produces loose clusters of lovely star-shaped blue flowers with white eyes.

Crocus chrysanthus 'E.A. Bowles'
CROCUS
☀ ❋❋❋ ↕ 7cm (3in) ↔ 5cm (2in)

This popular, spring-flowering crocus has slender green leaves, and lemon-yellow flowers, each with a bronze-green base and purple feathering on the outside. ▽

OTHER BULBS FOR SCREES AND ROCK GARDENS

Arum creticum, see p.32
Eucomis bicolor, see p.64
Iris bucharica
Iris magnifica
Ornithogalum arabicum
Pancratium illyricum, see p.41
Scilla peruviana, see p.33
Tulipa kaufmanniana
Tulipa humilis 'Violacea'
Urginea maritima

OTHER MINIATURE BULBS FOR
SCREES AND ROCK GARDENS

Allium mairei
Allium oreophilum
x *Chionoscilla allenii*
Crocus biflorus
Crocus chrysanthus 'Zwanenburg
  Bronze'
Iris 'Joyce'
Iris 'Katharine Hodgkin'
Muscari comosum
Narcissus triandrus

Iris danfordiae
MINIATURE IRIS
☀ ❄❄❄ ↕10cm (4in) ↔5cm (2in)

One of the most beautiful early bulbs, this
miniature iris has slim, four-angled leaves
and bears yellow flowers marked with
greenish yellow in late winter and spring.

Scilla bifolia
SCILLA
☀ ❄❄❄ ↕15cm (6in) ↔5cm (2in)

An easily grown bulb, which will increase
rapidly. It bears two narrow green leaves,
and loose sprays of star-shaped, blue to
purple-blue flowers in early spring. ♆

Narcissus minor
MINIATURE DAFFODIL
☀ ❄❄❄ ↕12.5cm (5in) ↔7.5cm (3in)

This little daffodil forms tufts or patches
of narrow, grey-green leaves. Its prettily
inclined, small yellow trumpet-flowers are
borne above the foliage in early spring. ♆

Puschkinia scilloides
PUSCHKINIA
☀ ❄❄❄ ↕15cm (6in) ↔7.5cm (3in)

Cheerful and reliable, this perennial soon
forms a small clump of slender leaves,
accompanied in spring by clusters of very
pale blue flowers with darker blue stripes.

Tulipa aucheriana
TULIP
☀ ❄❄❄ ↕25cm (10in) ↔15cm (6in)

Starry pink flowers, with yellow centres
and stamens, are borne singly or in twos or
threes during spring. The narrow, bloomy
green leaves are also attractive. ♆

Perennials for Wall or Rock Crevices and Paving

Rock crevices, especially in mountain areas, are the favoured habitat of a range of attractive perennials, which often have trailing or carpeting stems, or form small rosettes or hummocks. In the garden, these plants can be grown in the cracks of a dry stone wall, or between paving slabs, where they will get the good drainage they need.

S p e c i f i c   U s e s

Asarina procumbens
ASARINA
☼ ☼ ❄❄ ↕ 5cm (2in) ↔ 60cm (24in)

This free-growing evergreen has trailing, hairy stems. In summer, it produces pale yellow, snapdragon flowers from the axils of its kidney-shaped, grey-green leaves.

Aurinia saxatilis 'Dudley Nevill'
GOLD DUST
☼ ❄❄❄ ↕ 20cm (8in) ↔ 30cm (12in)

A popular, clump-forming, woody-based plant with evergreen, grey-green leaves, and clusters of tiny, soft yellow-buff flowers from late spring to early summer.

Convolvulus sabatius
CONVOLVULUS
☼ ❄❄ ↕ 15cm (6in) ↔ 60cm (24in)

The trailing, leafy stems of this carpeting, fast-growing perennial are studded with pale to deep lavender-blue flowers over many weeks in summer and autumn. ♔

Erigeron karvinskianus
MEXICAN FLEABANE
☼ ❄❄❄ ↕ 30cm (12in) ↔ 1m (3ft)

In summer, a succession of little white daisies, which fade to pink then purple, smother this charming plant's loose, airy clump of slender, branching stems. ♔

Aubrieta 'J.S. Baker'
AUBRETIA
☼ ❄❄❄ ↕ 5cm (2in) ↔ 60cm (24in)

Aubretias are among the most colourful and reliable evergreen perennials for walls or rock-work. This one is smothered with purple, white-eyed flowers during spring.

Campanula carpatica 'Jewel'
BELLFLOWER
☼ ☼ ❄❄❄ ↕ 10cm (4in) ↔ 45cm (18in)

The small, dense, heart-shaped leaves of this popular and attractive, compact bell-flower are almost hidden by its upturned, bright purple-blue blooms in summer.

OTHER HERBACEOUS PERENNIALS
FOR CREVICES AND PAVING

Anthemis marschalliana
Erinus alpinus
Erodium chrysanthum
Hypericum cerastioides
Incarvillea arguta
Origanum rotundifolium
Persicaria vacciniifolia, see p.44
Petrorhagia saxifraga
Phyteuma scheuchzeri
Saponaria 'Bressingham'

Gypsophila repens 'Dorothy Teacher'
GYPSOPHILA
☼ ❋❋❋ ↕5cm (2in) ↔40cm (16in)

Slender, crowded stems carpet the ground with small, narrow, semi-evergreen blue-green leaves. The tiny, pale pink flowers, borne in summer, darken with age. ♇

Saxifraga 'Southside Seedling'
SAXIFRAGE
☼☼ ❋❋❋ ↕30cm (12in) ↔20cm (8in)

The bold, arching sprays of red-spotted white flowers are a fine sight in late spring and early summer above the basal rosette of evergreen leaves. Also good in a trough.

> **OTHER EVERGREEN PERENNIALS FOR CREVICES AND PAVING**
>
> *Arabis* x *arendsii* 'Rosabella'
> *Corydalis lutea*, see p.82
> *Dianthus gratianopolitanus*
> *Erigeron glaucus*
> *Euphorbia myrsinites*
> *Lithodora diffusa* 'Heavenly Blue'
> *Onosma alborosea*
> *Phlox subulata*
> *Ramonda myconi*
> *Sempervivum* 'Othello'

Helianthemum 'Wisley White'
ROCK ROSE
☼ ❋❋❋ ↕25cm (10in) ↔45cm (18in)

This woody-based, evergreen perennial, or wide-spreading shrublet, bears creamy white, yellow-centred flowers over a long period from late spring into midsummer.

Haberlea rhodopensis 'Virginalis'
HABERLEA ☼ ☀
❋❋❋ ♇ ↕15cm (6in) ↔25cm (10in)

Loose umbels of funnel-shaped white flowers top the dense, evergreen clump of hairy, coarse-toothed leaves in late spring and summer. Charming for a shady wall.

Lewisia Cotyledon Hybrids
LEWISIA ☼☼
❋❋❋ ♇ ↕25cm (10in) ↔30cm (12in)

In late spring and early summer, loose heads of magenta-pink, yellow, or orange flowers rise above the rosette or clump of thick, wavy-margined, evergreen leaves.

Verbascum dumulosum
MULLEIN
☼ ❋❋❋ ↕25cm (10in) ↔40cm (16in)

An evergreen, woody-based perennial, or low subshrub, with downy, grey-green stems and leaves. Its rich yellow flowers are borne in late spring and summer. ♇

Perennials for Bog Gardens and Waterside Areas

A WEALTH OF ORNAMENTAL PERENNIALS are available for those fortunate enough to have water in their garden, even if it is only a wet, muddy depression. These plants rely on a constant supply of moisture for top performance, and include perennials with large or colourful flowers, as well as those with bold or even spectacular foliage.

Iris laevigata
IRIS

☀ ◐ ❄❄❄   ↕ 80cm (32in) ↔ 20cm (8in)

This famous iris from Japan has erect, grey-green leaves and single purple, blue, or white flowers borne in summer. It will grow in shallow water. ♗

OTHER FOLIAGE PERENNIALS FOR BOG & WATERSIDE GARDENS

Astilbe rivularis
Carex elata 'Aurea', see p.128
Gunnera manicata
Hosta 'Big Daddy', see p.122
Hosta 'Frances Williams'
Houttuynia cordata 'Chameleon', see p.62
Iris pseudacorus 'Variegata', see p.116
Matteuccia struthiopteris, see p.65
Petasites japonicus var. *giganteus*

Astilbe 'Purpurlanze'
ASTILBE

☀ ◐ ❄❄❄   ↕ 1.2m (4ft) ↔ 90cm (36in)

The English name 'Purple Lance' aptly describes the stiff, purple-pink flower panicles of this late-flowering astilbe. Its deeply divided leaves form bold clumps.

Filipendula palmata 'Rubra'
FILIPENDULA

☀ ❄❄❄   ↕ 1.2m (4ft) ↔ 60cm (24in)

Sometimes confused with *F. rubra*, this stately, clump-forming perennial produces boldly lobed or divided leaves and dense plumes of tiny, rose-red summer flowers.

Darmera peltata
UMBRELLA PLANT

☀ ◐ ❄❄❄   ↕ 1.1m (3½ft) ↔ 75cm (30in)

This handsome perennial has creeping rhizomes that form a large patch of long-stalked leaves, colouring richly in autumn. Pink flowerheads are borne in spring. ♗

Hosta 'Zounds'
PLANTAIN LILY

☀ ◐ ❄❄❄   ↕ 55cm (22in) ↔ 1m (3ft)

Striking and relatively slug-proof, this hosta forms a big clump of boldly veined and dimpled, rounded leaves. In summer, the greenish yellow foliage ages to yellow.

Lysichiton americanus
YELLOW SKUNK CABBAGE

☀ ◐ ❄❄❄   ↕ 1m (3ft) ↔ 1.2m (4ft)

This has to be one of the most spectacular and easily recognized plants. It bears large yellow flowers in spring, followed by huge clumps of paddle-shaped leaves. ♗

Oenanthe javanica 'Flamingo'
WATER DROPWORT
☼ ☼ ✳✳✳ ↕ 40cm (16in) ↔ 90cm (36in)

The deeply cut, green and white leaves of
this creeping, fleshy-stemmed perennial
become pink flushed in autumn. Small
white flowerheads emerge in late summer.

Osmunda regalis
ROYAL FERN
☼ ☼ ✳✳✳ ↕ 1.5m (5ft) ↔ 1.2m (4ft)

An impressive fern, forming a bold clump
of deeply divided fronds that often colour
richly in autumn before dying. It produces
spikes of red-brown spores in summer. ♔

Rheum palmatum 'Bowles Crimson'
ORNAMENTAL RHUBARB
☼ ☼ ✳✳✳ ↕ 2.5m (8ft) ↔ 1.8m (6ft)

The big, jaggedly lobed leaves of this
spectacular perennial emerge crimson and
form a giant clump. Statuesque panicles of
red flowers are produced in early summer.

**OTHER FLOWERING PERENNIALS
FOR BOG & WATERSIDE GARDENS**

Euphorbia palustris
Eupatorium purpureum
  'Atropurpureum', see p.18
Filipendula purpurea, see p.122
Iris ensata
Ligularia dentata 'Othello'
Lysichiton camtschatcensis
Lythrum salicaria 'Blush'
Mimulus cardinalis
Primula pulverulenta

Primula prolifera
CANDELABRA PRIMULA
☼ ☼ ✳✳✳ ↕ 60cm (24in) ↔ 15cm (6in)

In early summer, slender, erect stems with
many whorls of yellow flowers rise above
the basal rosettes of deep green leaves. It
is excellent for planting in drifts. ♔

Rodgersia pinnata
RODGERSIA
☼ ☼ ✳✳✳ ↕ 1.2m (4ft) ↔ 75cm (30in)

Superb for both foliage and flowers, with
its deeply divided, veined leaves, tinted
red in autumn and spring, and its frothy
white flower plumes borne in summer.

Zantedeschia aethiopica 'Crowborough'
EASTER LILY
☼ ☼ ✳✳✳ ↕ 90cm (36in) ↔ 60cm (24in)

Also called Lily of the Nile, this handsome
perennial has large, arrow-shaped leaves,
and beautiful, long-stalked white flowers
in summer. It will grow in shallow water.

Aquatic Perennials

THERE ARE VERY FEW RICHER, or more ornamental, wildlife habitats in the garden than in and around a well-planted pond or pool. Aquatic perennials will attract a varied fauna, and although large ponds offer the most scope for planting, water can be introduced into even the smallest backyard or town garden using containers. The planting depths below indicate the depth of water required; plant heights are from water level.

Nymphaea 'Firecrest'
WATER LILY
☼ ❄❄❄ ↕ 7.5cm (3in) ↔ 1.2m (4ft)

This water lily's rounded, floating leaves are purple when young. Its fragrant pink flowers open in summer. Ideal for a small pond. Plant 15–45cm (6–18in) deep.

Aponogeton distachyos
WATER HAWTHORN
☼ ☼ ❄❄ ↕ 7.5cm (3in) ↔ 1.2m (4ft)

In spring and autumn, deliciously vanilla-scented white flower spikes rise above the floating, semi-evergreen, oblong leaves. Plant in water 30–60cm (12–24in) deep.

Houttuynia cordata 'Chameleon'
HOUTTUYNIA
☼ ☼ ❄❄❄ ↕ 30cm (12in) ↔ indefinite

A low-spreading, marginal aquatic plant for water to 10cm (4in) deep, or moist soil. The orange-peel-scented leaves have pale yellow, green, and red variegation.

Nymphaea 'Gladstoniana'
WATER LILY
☼ ❄❄❄ ↕ 7.5cm (3in) ↔ 2.4m (8ft)

This popular, vigorous water lily has starry white flowers in summer, and rounded, wavy-edged, floating leaves, bronze when young. Plant 45–90cm (18–36in) deep. ♔

Butomus umbellatus
FLOWERING RUSH
☼ ❄❄❄ ↕ 1.2m (4ft) ↔ 45cm (18in)

A robust plant for pond margins, forming a patch of long, three-cornered leaves. Tall stems bear umbels of rose-pink flowers in summer. Plant 7–13cm (3–5in) deep. ♔

Nymphaea 'Chromatella'
WATER LILY
☼ ❄❄❄ ↕ 7.5cm (3in) ↔ 1.5m (5ft)

Free-flowering and vigorous, this reliable plant has beautiful, canary-yellow flowers in summer, and bronze-splashed floating leaves. Plant 45–90cm (18–36in) deep. ♔

Nymphoides peltata
WATER FRINGE
☼ ❄❄❄ ↕ 7.5cm (3in) ↔ indefinite

Ideal for a large pond, this fast-spreader has rounded, floating leaves, and golden, funnel-shaped, fringe-petalled flowers in summer. Plant 30–60cm (12–24in) deep.

Orontium aquaticum
GOLDEN CLUB

☼ ❄❄❄   ↕ 30cm (12in) ↔ 60cm (24in)

A vigorous marginal aquatic with oblong, blue-green leaves, and curved white stalks bearing yellow flower spikes from summer to autumn. Plant 30–40cm (12–16in) deep.

Pontederia cordata
PICKEREL WEED

☼ ❄❄   ↕ 75cm (30in) ↔ 60cm (24in)

During late summer, dense spikes of blue flowers poke through the clumps of erect, glossy leaves. Plant this vigorous marginal aquatic 7–13cm (3–5in) deep. 🏆

Sagittaria latifolia
DUCK POTATO

☼ ❄❄❄   ↕↔ 90cm (36in)

A tuberous marginal aquatic with slender, triangular stems and arrow-shaped, long-stalked leaves. In summer, whorls of white flowers open. Plant 7–13cm (3–5in) deep.

Stratiotes aloides
WATER SOLDIER

☼ ❄❄❄   ↕ 15cm (6in) ↔ 20cm (8in)

Pineapple-like rosettes of saw-toothed leaves rise to the water surface in summer, as the erect, three-petalled white flowers are borne. Plant 30–90cm (12–36in) deep.

OTHER AQUATIC PERENNIALS

Acorus gramineus
Alisma plantago-aquatica
Calla palustris
Cyperus eragrostis
Hottonia palustris
Hydrocharis morsus-ranae
Iris laevigata, see p.60
Menyanthes trifoliata
Mimulus ringens
Myriophyllum verticillatum
Nuphar lutea
Nymphaea 'Escarboucle'
Nymphaea 'Gonnère'
Nymphaea 'James Brydon'
Peltandra sagittifolia
Ranunculus aquatilis
Utricularia vulgaris
Zantedeschia aethiopica 'Crowborough', see p.61

Typha minima
SMALL REEDMACE

☼ ❄❄❄   ↕ 75cm (30in) ↔ 45cm (18in)

A rush-like marginal aquatic with slender leaves. The stems of brown flowerheads in summer turn into fluffy seed heads in winter. Plant 5–10cm (2–4in) deep.

Perennials for Containers in Sun

ONE OF THE MAIN ADVANTAGES of growing perennials in containers is that they can easily be moved around the garden or patio, just like furniture inside the house. Containers also allow less hardy plants, like some of the sun-lovers below, to be grown outdoors for summer effect, then moved under cover for protection in winter.

SPECIFIC USES

Agapanthus 'Loch Hope'
AFRICAN LILY
☼ ❄❄❄   ↕1.2m (4ft) ↔60cm (24in)

This bold, clump-forming lily is hardy outside in all but the coldest areas. Deep blue trumpet-flowers are carried in loose heads from late summer into autumn. ♔

Canna 'Assaut'
INDIAN SHOT
☼ ❄   ↕1.5m (5ft) ↔50cm (20in)

A striking perennial with bold, purple-brown leaves and stout, erect, leafy stems that bear heads of gladiolus-like, orange-scarlet flowers in summer and autumn.

Osteospermum 'Silver Sparkler'
OSTEOSPERMUM
☼ ❄   ↕60cm (24in) ↔45cm (18in)

This vigorous, bushy plant has creamy-white-margined leaves. Dark shoots bear long-stalked white daisy-flowers, darker on the reverse, from summer into autumn.

> **OTHER PERENNIALS FOR CONTAINERS IN SUN**
>
> *Agapanthus campanulatus* 'Albovittatus'
> *Argyranthemum* 'Vancouver'
> *Begonia sutherlandii*, see p.40
> *Bidens ferulifolia*
> *Francoa sonchifolia*, see p.27
> *Hedychium gardnerianum*, see p.41
> *Lotus berthelotii*
> *Rehmannia elata*
> *Salvia gesneriiflora*
> *Sedum sieboldii* 'Mediovariegatum'

Argyranthemum 'Jamaica Primrose'
ARGYRANTHEMUM
☼ ❄   ↕↔1m (3ft)

A bushy evergreen with slender stems and fine-cut, grey-green leaves. Long-stalked, primrose-yellow daisies are borne over a long period from spring into autumn. ♔

Eucomis bicolor
PINEAPPLE FLOWER
☼ ❄❄❄   ↕45cm (18in) ↔30cm (12in)

The dense, beautiful but curious heads of pale green, purple-edged flowers have pineapple-like crowns, and rise over strap-shaped, fleshy leaves in late summer.

Verbena x *hybrida* 'Peaches and Cream'
VERBENA
☼ ❄   ↕45cm (18in) ↔50cm (20in)

In summer, the mound of toothed, rough-hairy, dark green leaves is covered by domed heads of pale orange-pink flowers, which age to apricot- then creamy yellow.

Perennials for Containers in Shade

SHADY PATIOS, BACKYARDS, and similar sunless situations, particularly when paved or close to the house, are not always the easiest places to accommodate plants unless they are grown in containers. Foliage perennials are especially useful in shade, and while many also bear attractive flowers, they are striking as specimens, or grouped, in containers.

OTHER PERENNIALS FOR
CONTAINERS IN SHADE

Bergenia cordifolia 'Purpurea', see p.114
Dryopteris erythrosora, see p.140
Hakonechloa macra 'Aureola', see p.124
Helleborus argutifolius, see p.114
Heuchera 'Pewter Moon'
Hosta 'Zounds', see p.60
Lilium longiflorum
Saxifraga fortunei 'Rubrifolia'
Tolmiea menziesii 'Taff's Gold',
  see p.125

Aspidistra elatior
ASPIDISTRA, CAST-IRON PLANT
☼ ☀ ❄❄   ↕ ↔ 60cm (24in)

Thriving in shade, this old favourite for parlours always looks in good health with its broad, strap-shaped, beautifully veined and glossy, evergreen foliage.

Hosta 'Sum and Substance'
PLANTAIN LILY
☼ ☀ ❄❄❄❄   ↕ 75cm (30in) ↔ 90cm (36in)

One of the best hostas for brightening a shady corner, with its bold clump of heart-shaped, yellow-green to yellow leaves. It bears pale lilac flowers in summer.

Matteucia struthiopteris
SHUTTLECOCK FERN
☼ ❄❄❄   ↕ 1.2m (4ft) ↔ 50cm (20in)

The bold, elegant shuttlecock of laddered fronds surrounds a central cluster of dark brown, spore-bearing fronds from late summer on. It needs moist compost.

Corydalis flexuosa
'China Blue'
☼ ❄❄❄   ↕ 25cm (10in) ↔ 20cm (8in)

Worth growing just for its attractive, ferny, bright green winter foliage, which dies down in early summer as the racemes of tubular, striking blue flowers fade.

Liriope muscari
LILYTURF
☼ ☀ ❄❄❄❄   ↕ 30cm (12in) ↔ 45cm (18in)

Dense tufts of evergreen, strap-shaped, dark green leaves are joined in autumn by stiff, crowded spikes of violet-mauve flowers. Good for ground cover too.

Rodgersia pinnata 'Superba'
RODGERSIA
☼ ☼ ☀ ❄❄❄❄   ↕ 1.2m (4ft) ↔ 75cm (30in)

This vigorous clump-former has the dual attractions of bold, fingered, veiny leaves, bronze-purple when young, and conical, rich pink flower plumes in summer.

Climbing Perennials

OST CLIMBING PERENNIALS cultivated in the garden are woody-stemmed and have a permanent presence above ground. There are, however, a surprising number of herbaceous perennials that have twining or scrambling stems ideal for clothing walls, fences, and trellis, or for training over shrubs and trees or similar supports. As well as flowers and foliage, some also offer decorative fruits and seed heads, or richly tinted autumn leaves.

SPECIFIC USES

OTHER CLIMBING PERENNIALS

Aconitum hemsleyanum
Aconitum volubile
Calystegia hederacea 'Flore Pleno'
Clematis x *eriostemon*
Lathyrus latifolius 'Blushing Bride'
Lathyrus nervosus
Lathyrus rotundifolius
Tropaeolum ciliatum
Tropaeolum tuberosum
Tropaeolum tuberosum var.
  lineamaculatum 'Ken Aslet'

Clematis x *durandii*
CLEMATIS
☼ ❋❋ ↕ 2m (6ft) ↔ 1m (3ft)

Perfect for ground cover or training over a small bush, the slender stems bear single summer flowers with creamy stamens and wide-spaced, indigo-blue tepals. ♔

Lathyrus grandiflorus
EVERLASTING PEA
☼ ☀ ❋❋❋ ↕ ↔ 1.5m (5ft)

An old cottage-garden favourite, providing dense cover with its rampant, slender stems. Long-stalked clusters of pink, red, and purple flowers open in summer. ♔

Humulus lupulus 'Aureus'
GOLDEN HOP
☼ ☀ ❋❋❋❋ ↕ ↔ 6m (20ft)

The twining stems of this powerful, fast-growing climber blanket its support with golden yellow leaves. Bunches of greenish yellow seed heads appear in autumn. ♔

Lathyrus latifolius 'Albus'
PERENNIAL PEA
☼ ☀ ❋❋❋❋ ↕ ↔ 2m (6ft)

Easy and reliable, this strong-growing scrambler is ideal for a wall or hedge, or for covering a steep bank. In summer and autumn, it produces white pea-flowers.

Tropaeolum speciosum
FLAME CREEPER
☼ ☀ ❋❋❋ PH ↕ ↔ 3m (10ft)

Spectacular when in flower in summer and autumn, the long-spurred, flame-red blooms are followed by blue fruits with red collars. It requires cool, moist soil. ♔

Perennials with Leaves Suitable for Cutting

I N THE HOME, AS IN THE GARDEN, foliage is as important and decorative as flowers. Many perennials can provide a regular and reliable supply of attractive leaves for cutting whenever required. Useful for adding a green, grey, or golden foil to flower arrangements, cut leaves will also make an effective display by themselves.

SPECIFIC USES

Paeonia 'Edulis Superba'
PEONY
☼ ☀ ❄❄❄ ↕ ↔ 90cm (36in)

Most herbaceous peonies have attractive, rich green foliage with contrasting red or purplish stalks. This one also has double pink flowers that are excellent for cutting.

OTHER PERENNIALS WITH LEAVES SUITABLE FOR CUTTING

Arum italicum 'Marmoratum', see p.135
Astilbe 'Fanal'
Bergenia cordifolia 'Purpurea', see p.114
Galax urceolata
Hakonechloa macra 'Aureola', see p.124
Hosta 'Shade Master'
Hosta 'Zounds', see p.60
Phormium tenax, see p.117
Polygonatum multiflorum 'Striatum'
Polystichum munitum, see p.140
Rodgersia pinnata, see p.61

Hosta 'Hadspen Blue'
PLANTAIN LILY
☼ ☀ ❄❄❄ ↕ 25cm (10in) ↔ 60cm (24in)

Hostas are invaluable for cut foliage, and those with blue-grey leaves are especially useful. This exceptional example has handsome bold, heart-shaped leaves.

Hosta 'Green Fountain'
PLANTAIN LILY
☼ ☀ ❄❄❄ ↕ 45cm (18in) ↔ 1m (3ft)

This hosta's arching, lance-shaped, wavy-margined, glossy leaves form a bold clump, and are ideal for picking. Arching stems bear pale mauve flowers in summer.

Iris pallida 'Argentea Variegata'
IRIS
☼ ☀ ❄❄❄ ↕ 80cm (32in) ↔ 60cm (24in)

One of the most spectacular variegated perennials, with sword-shaped, boldly margined leaves lasting long into autumn. Fragrant flowers open in early summer.

Polygonatum falcatum 'Variegatum'
SOLOMON'S SEAL
☼ ☀ ❄❄❄ ↕ 60cm (24in) ↔ 30cm (12in)

In time, this charming perennial forms a clump of arching reddish shoots, with rich green, cream-margined leaves. In spring, it bears clusters of pendent bell-flowers.

Perennials for Cut Flowers

T HE AVAILABILITY OF CUT FLOWERS for home decoration is one of the most enjoyable bonuses of growing perennials. Cutting, preferably from well-established plants, should be selective, leaving most of the clumps virtually intact, while providing enough flowers for an arrangement. Although some perennials, such as asters, have long been popular among florists, many more bear flowers suitable for cutting. Once cut, stand the flowers in a container of water overnight before use.

Astilbe 'Professor van der Wielen'
ASTILBE
☼ ☀ ❆❆❆   ↕ 1.2m (4ft) ↔ 1m (3ft)

One of the boldest and most satisfying astilbes for cool, moist soil. In summer, tall, arching plumes of tiny white flowers rise over mounds of much-divided leaves.

Catananche caerulea
BLUE CUPIDONE
☼ ❆❆❆   ↕ 80cm (32in) ↔ 30cm (12in)

The slender clusters of erect, wiry stems are tipped in summer with papery, pearly white buds, opening to blue cornflowers. The flowers are also attractive when dried.

Aquilegia McKana Hybrids
COLUMBINE
☼ ☀ ❆❆❆ ↕ 75cm (30in) ↔ 60cm (24in)

This striking but short-lived perennial produces its large, long-spurred flowers in shades of blue, yellow, and red from late spring through to midsummer.

OTHER SPRING-FLOWERING PERENNIALS FOR CUT FLOWERS

Bergenia 'Beethoven', see p.26
Convallaria majalis
Doronicum x *excelsum* 'Harpur Crewe'
Galanthus 'Atkinsii', see p.82
Narcissus 'Actaea'
Narcissus 'Mount Hood', see p.85
Polygonatum x *hybridum*
Primula vulgaris
Tulipa 'Purissima'
Viola odorata

Aster x *frikartii* 'Wunder von Stäfa'
ASTER
☼ ❆❆❆   ↕ 70cm (28in) ↔ 40cm (16in)

A reliable plant for a late summer or early autumn border, with a multitude of long-lasting blue, orange-centred daisies. Its stems may flop if not given support. ♗

Gaillardia 'Kobold'
BLANKET FLOWER
☼ ❆❆❆   ↕ 30cm (12in) ↔ 45cm (18in)

Also known as 'Goblin', this downy, bushy plant is relatively short-lived, but displays large, brilliant red, yellow-tipped daisy-flowers during summer and early autumn.

Iris unguicularis 'Mary Barnard'
IRIS
☀ ❄❄❄   ↕ 30cm (12in) ↔ 60cm (24in)

The fragrant, solitary flowers of this sun-loving iris appear from late winter to early spring, and are best picked when in bud. Its evergreen leaves form a grassy clump.

Lilium 'African Queen'
TRUMPET LILY
☀ ☀ ❄❄❄   ↕ 1.5m (5ft) ↔ 30cm (12in)

Most lilies are good for cutting, and this is no exception. Its tall stems bear narrow, crowded leaves, and terminal umbels of fragrant, nodding flowers in summer.

Schizostylis coccinea 'Viscountess Byng'
KAFFIR LILY
☀ ❄❄❄   ↕ 60cm (24in) ↔ 30cm (12in)

A very useful autumn-flowering perennial, forming a clump, or in time a patch, of narrow, iris-like leaves, and bearing loose spikes of star-shaped, pale pink flowers.

Leucanthemum × *superbum* 'Cobham Gold'
☀ ☀ ❄❄❄   ↕ 60cm (24in) ↔ 20cm (8in)

This lovely selection is one of the shasta daisies, which are all excellent for cutting. It forms robust clumps, with double white flowers during summer and early autumn.

OTHER SUMMER-FLOWERING PERENNIALS FOR CUT FLOWERS

Agapanthus 'Blue Giant', see p.84
Achillea 'Coronation Gold', see p.102
Alstroemeria Ligtu Hybrids
Crocosmia masoniorum, see p.104
Dianthus 'Doris', see p.110
Echinacea purpurea
Gypsophila paniculata 'Bristol Fairy', see p.93
Paeonia 'Sarah Bernhardt', see p.107
Platycodon grandiflorus, see p.77

Liatris spicata 'Kobold'
GAYFEATHER
☀ ❄❄❄   ↕ 50cm (20in) ↔ 45cm (18in)

A striking and reliable perennial for moist but well-drained soils. It forms a clump of slender leaves, with erect, dense purple flower spikes in late summer and autumn.

Paeonia officinalis 'Crimson Globe'
PEONY
☀ ❄❄❄❄   ↕ 85cm (34in) ↔ 90cm (36in)

This bold, clump-forming peony produces handsome, divided, deep green foliage. The large, single, garnet-red blooms, with golden yellow stamens, appear in summer.

Solidago 'Laurin'
GOLDEN ROD
☀ ❄❄❄   ↕ 75cm (30in) ↔ 45cm (18in)

This compact version of an old-fashioned, cottage-garden stalwart bears branched, spreading heads of deep yellow flowers on clumps of leafy stems in late summer.

Perennials with Decorative Winter Seed Heads

MOST GARDENERS NOW RECOGNIZE that taking too tidy an approach to the garden at the end of the growing season can rob them of some striking winter effects. Any perennial that has a dried superstructure of seed heads can provide attractive winter interest, and their architectural beauty will be further enhanced by a covering of snow or hoar frost.

Achillea filipendulina
ACHILLEA
☼ ❄❄❄ ↕1.2m (4ft) ↔45cm (18in)

The flattened seed heads of this clump-forming, stiff-stemmed perennial provide a ready platform for snow or hoar frost. Its yellow flowers are produced in summer.

Echinops ritro
GLOBE THISTLE
☼ ☼ ❄❄❄❄ ↕60cm (24in) ↔45cm (18in)

When covered in frost, the globular, spiky seed heads of this easy-to-grow perennial look like decorative baubles. The flowers emerge bright blue in late spring. ♛

Miscanthus sinensis 'Kleine Fontäne'
MISCANTHUS
☼ ❄❄❄ ↕1.5m (5ft) ↔1.2m (4ft)

In autumn, handsome clumps of tall, erect stems, with narrow leaves, bear finger-like spikelets, which turn fluffy and from buff to white in winter. Ideal for small gardens.

OTHER PERENNIALS WITH DECORATIVE WINTER SEED HEADS

Astilbe 'Superba'
Cimicifuga simplex
Eupatorium purpureum
  'Atropurpureum', see p.18
Filipendula rubra 'Venusta'
Iris sibirica
Monarda 'Anja'
Panicum squamosum
Sedum spectabile, see p.102

Chasmanthium latifolium
SPANGLE GRASS
☼ ☼ ❄❄❄ ↕1m (3ft) ↔60cm (24in)

This gorgeous grass forms loose clumps of leafy stems, which bear lax or drooping clusters of flattened, green or pink-tinted spikelets, turning pale brown in winter.

Gypsophila paniculata
'Compacta Plena'
☼ ❄❄❄ ↕30cm (12in) ↔60cm (24in)

A compact, dwarf form of the well-known baby's breath (*G. paniculata*). The small, double, soft pink to white flowers create a spangled effect when covered in frost.

Monarda 'Beauty of Cobham'
BERGAMOT
☼ ☼ ❄❄❄ ↕90cm (36in) ↔45cm (18in)

Flowering during late summer and early autumn, this lovely plant bears crowded heads of pink flowers, with purple bracts that turn a warm brown in winter. ♛

Stipa tenuissima
FEATHER GRASS
☀ ✳✳✳　　　　　　　$\updownarrow$ ↔ 60cm (24in)

A densely tufted grass with ever-moving, erect then arching stems. These bear long, feathery heads of green-white spikelets, which turn a warm buff colour in winter.

Phlomis tuberosa
PHLOMIS
☀ ✳✳✳　　　$\updownarrow$ 1.5m (5ft) ↔ 90cm (36in)

Throughout winter, the striking clumps of tall, leafless stems carry dense brown seed heads. Two-lipped, rose-lilac flowers with reddish calyces are produced in summer.

Phlox 'Lichtspel'
BORDER PHLOX
☀ ✳✳✳　　　$\updownarrow$ 1.2m (4ft) ↔ 60cm (24in)

During summer, the clumps of erect, leafy stems carry panicles of lilac-rose flowers. The stems and remaining flowerheads fade to a warm pale brown during winter.

Rhaponticum cynarioides
RHAPONTICUM
☀ ✳✳✳　　　$\updownarrow$ 75cm (30in) ↔ 30cm (12in)

Erect stems rise from a basal rosette of lobed leaves in summer to carry large cornflower heads of pink flowers, which turn brown and persist throughout winter.

Veronicastrum virginicum
CULVER'S ROOT
☀ ☀ ✳✳✳　　　$\updownarrow$ 2m (6ft) ↔ 45cm (18in)

Tapered spikes of blue-purple flowers top dense clumps of erect stems, with whorled leaves, in summer and autumn. In winter, the spikes lengthen and turn brown.

Perennials Attractive to Bees, Butterflies, and Other Insects

OTHER PERENNIALS ATTRACTIVE
TO BEES AND BUTTERFLIES

Achillea 'Moonshine'
Allium 'Globemaster', see p.82
Asclepias incarnata
Aster amellus 'Veilchenkönigin',
  see p.94
Centranthus ruber, see p.86
Eryngium x *tripartitum*, see p.31
Eupatorium purpureum
  'Atropurpureum', see p.18
Monarda 'Squaw', see p.105

COLOURFUL BUTTERFLIES are always welcome visitors to our gardens, but many other less decorative insects in fact have more important roles to play. These include bees, which are essential as garden pollinators, and also hoverflies, whose larvae feed on aphids and act as a form of natural pest control. They will all be attracted by the following perennials.

Allium 'Purple Sensation'
ORNAMENTAL ONION
☼ ❄❄❄   ↕ 90cm (36in) ↔ 10cm (4in)

All the alliums are attractive to insects but this one is particularly impressive. The tall stems carry spangled globes of starry, deep violet flowers during summer. ▽

Centaurea 'Pulchra Major'
CENTAUREA
☼ ❄❄❄   ↕ 1.2m (4ft) ↔ 60cm (24in)

This bold clump-former has handsome, silver-grey foliage. During summer, erect, branching stems bear striking, rose-pink flowerheads with scaly, silvery bracts.

Calamintha nepeta 'White Cloud'
LESSER CALAMINT
☼ ☼ ❄❄❄   ↕ 45cm (18in) ↔ 75cm (30in)

Bees especially love this small-flowered perennial. Throughout summer, the low mound of crowded, aromatic leaves is peppered with tiny, pure white blooms.

Cephalaria gigantea
GIANT SCABIOUS
☼ ☼ ❄❄❄   ↕ 2.5m (8ft) ↔ 90cm (36in)

A special favourite with bees, this giant scabious produces clumps of deeply lobed leaves, and tall, branched stems carrying primrose-yellow flowerheads in summer.

Doronicum pardalianches
LEOPARD'S BANE
☼ ❄❄❄   ↕ 90cm (36in) ↔ 1.2m (4ft)

In time, this creeping perennial will form a substantial patch of heart-shaped, softly-hairy leaves. Yellow daisy-heads are borne over a long period in spring and summer.

Salvia pratensis Haematodes Group
MEADOW CLARY
☼ ◐ ✳✳✳ ↕90cm (36in) ↔ 30cm (12in)

Short-lived but free-seeding, this meadow clary produces large, branching heads of blue-violet flowers in summer, above rosettes of aromatic, large green leaves.

Echinops ritro 'Veitch's Blue'
GLOBE THISTLE
☼ ◐ ✳✳✳ ↕1.2m (4ft) ↔ 75cm (30in)

During summer, the spherical, spiky blue flowerheads make this a favourite with both children and bees. Its spine-toothed, deep-cut leaves are white-downy beneath.

Lavandula stoechas
FRENCH LAVENDER
☼ ✳✳✳ ↕↔60cm (24in)

Bushy, with a dense, compact habit, this aromatic evergreen has narrow, grey-green leaves, and long-stalked spikes of purple flowers in late spring and summer. ♈

Sedum 'Herbstfreude'
ICE PLANT
☼ ✳✳✳ ↕↔60cm (24in)

Often known as *S.* 'Autumn Joy', this will lure butterflies and bees with its deep pink autumn flowers, maturing copper-red. Its fleshy leaves are grey-bloomy. ♈

Inula hookeri
INULA
☼ ✳✳✳ ↕↔90cm (36in)

One of the best plants for attracting bees to the garden. The bold clumps of downy, leafy stems produce golden daisy-heads from woolly buds in summer and autumn.

Melittis melissophyllum
BASTARD BALM
☼ ◐ ✳✳✳ ↕↔30cm (12in)

This softly-downy balm has four-angled stems and honey-scented leaves. Loved by bees, the purple-lipped, white to pink flowers open in spring and early summer.

Solidago 'Goldenmosa'
GOLDEN ROD
☼ ✳✳✳ ↕1m (3ft) ↔ 60cm (24in)

A compact, bushy perennial with erect, leafy stems, and conical heads of bright yellow flowerheads from late summer into autumn. Ideal for smaller gardens. ♈

Perennials Tolerant of Air Pollution

AIR POLLUTION FROM ANY SOURCE can have a detrimental effect on plants, and severe or prolonged exposure may ultimately cause plant deaths. Fortunately, such cases are the exception rather than the rule, and the following perennials can generally be relied on to tolerate all but the most extreme conditions found in industrial areas or roadside sites.

Achillea ptarmica 'The Pearl'
SNEEZEWORT
☼ ❄❄❄   ↕75cm (30in) ↔60cm (24in)

This well-proven, tough perennial forms clumps of aromatic, narrow, toothy leaves. The dense heads of button-like white flowers are produced in summer.

Aster novae-angliae 'Andenken an Alma Pötschke'
☼ ☼ ❄❄❄   ↕1.2m (4ft) ↔60cm (24in)

Often known simply as 'Alma Pötschke', this clump-forming michaelmas daisy lights up the early autumn days with its brilliant salmon-pink daisy-flowers. ♈

Geranium pratense 'Plenum Caeruleum'
☼ ☼ ❄❄❄   ↕90cm (36in) ↔60cm (24in)

All forms of this well-known cranesbill are reliable. This strong-growing selection produces attractive, small, loosely double, lavender-blue flowers during summer.

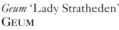

Geum 'Lady Stratheden'
GEUM
☼ ☼ ❄❄❄   ↕↔60cm (24in)

An old favourite, and a contrast to scarlet *G.* 'Mrs. Bradshaw', with loose sprays of semi-double, rich yellow summer flowers, and deeply divided, fresh green leaves. ♈

Leucanthemum × *superbum* 'Esther Read'
☼ ❄❄❄   ↕↔60cm (24in)

The large, double, pure white flowerheads of this reliable, summer-blooming shasta daisy are good for cutting. Its leafy stems form broad clumps.

Lupinus 'My Castle'
LUPIN
☼ ❄❄❄   ↕90cm (36in) ↔75cm (30in)

In summer, the bold clump of erect stems and finger-like leaves is topped by long spires of deep rose-pink pea-flowers. It needs protection where slugs abound.

OTHER FLOWERING PERENNIALS TOLERANT OF AIR POLLUTION

Anaphalis margaritacea var. *yedoensis*
Anemone hupehensis 'September Charm', see p.96
Dicentra 'Spring Morning'
Geranium × *magnificum*
Liatris spicata
Lupinus 'The Chatelaine'
Lychnis chalcedonica
Sidalcea candida
Solidago 'Laurin', see p.69

OTHER FOLIAGE PERENNIALS
TOLERANT OF AIR POLLUTION

Acanthus mollis Latifolius Group
Artemisia ludoviciana 'Silver Queen', see p.86
Bergenia cordifolia 'Purpurea', see p.114
Crambe cordifolia, see p.22
Cynara cardunculus, see p.130
Lamium galeobdolon 'Florentinum', see p.47
Macleaya × kewensis 'Flamingo'
Myrrhis odorata, see p.49

SPECIFIC USES

Lupinus 'Noble Maiden'
LUPIN
☀ ❄❄❄   ↕ 90cm (36in) ↔ 75cm (30in)

A lovely lupin, with tapered racemes of creamy white pea-flowers in summer, rising above the clump of divided foliage. Like most lupins, it is attractive to slugs.

Pentaglottis sempervirens
GREEN ALKANET
☀ ☀ ❄❄❄   ↕ 90cm (36in) ↔ 60cm (24in)

The robust clump of overwintering, hairy leaves is joined in spring by erect, leafy stems bearing rich blue, bird's-eye flowers. Excellent for hedge bottoms or woodland.

Solidago 'Golden Wings'
GOLDEN ROD
☀ ❄❄❄   ↕ 1.8m (6ft) ↔ 90cm (36in)

During late summer and autumn, the erect, leafy stems of this robust perennial are crowned with spreading, branched heads of golden yellow flower clusters.

Malva moschata
MUSK MALLOW
☀ ❄❄❄   ↕ 90cm (36in) ↔ 60cm (24in)

Attractive and easily grown, this perennial forms clumps of finely divided, aromatic leaves and bears racemes of pink mallow flowers from midsummer onwards.

Potentilla 'Gibson's Scarlet'
POTENTILLA
☀ ❄❄❄   ↕ 45cm (18in) ↔ 60cm (24in)

Popular for borders and striking in flower, this potentilla produces its bright scarlet blooms in summer above clumps of long-stalked, deeply divided leaves.   ♆

Veronica spicata 'Rotfuchs'
VERONICA
☀ ❄❄❄   ↕ ↔ 30cm (12in)

Erect, tapering spikes of eye-catching, deep pink flowers tower above the low clump of willow-like leaves in summer. Its German name means 'Red Fox'.

Perennials Tolerant of Coastal Exposure

EXPOSURE TO STRONG WINDS, SALT SPRAY, AND SUN are the three main features of life by the seaside. As the soil here is also often sandy or shingly and free-draining, plants must be both robust and adaptable to survive. A surprising number of perennials can cope successfully with these conditions and are ideal for a coastal garden.

Euphorbia nicaeensis
SPURGE
☼ ✳✳✳   ↕ 80cm (32in) ↔ 45cm (18in)

This superb evergreen plant is valued for its reddish green stems and narrow, blue-bloomy leaves. Green-yellow flowerheads are borne in late spring and summer.

Cichorium intybus 'Roseum'
CHICORY
☼ ✳✳✳   ↕ 1.2m (4ft) ↔ 60cm (24in)

A tap-rooted perennial producing a clump of jaggedly lobed and toothed leaves. Spikes of dandelion-like pink flowerheads are carried on branched stems in summer.

Geranium sanguineum 'Max Frei'
BLOODY CRANESBILL
☼ ✳✳✳   ↕ 20cm (8in) ↔ 30cm (12in)

The neat, rounded hummocks of deeply cut, evergreen leaves are often richly red-tinted in autumn. A mass of deep magenta flowers emerges throughout summer.

Allium giganteum
ORNAMENTAL ONION
☼ ✳✳✳   ↕ 1.5m (5ft) ↔ 15cm (6in)

Round heads of starry, lilac-pink flowers top the tall stems of this striking plant in summer. Its two strap-shaped, grey-green basal leaves wither before flowering.

Centaurea hypoleuca 'John Coutts'
CENTAUREA
☼ ✳✳✳   ↕ 60cm (24in) ↔ 45cm (18in)

In summer, erect stems bear long-lasting, fragrant, deep rose-pink cornflower-heads above bold clumps of deeply lobed, wavy-margined leaves, grey-white beneath.

Erigeron 'Charity'
FLEABANE
☼ ☼ ✳✳✳   ↕ 60cm (24in) ↔ 45cm (18in)

Leafy clumps of stems produce cheerful, lilac-pink, yellow-centred daisy-heads, singly or in clusters, during summer. The flowers are a favourite with bees.

Glaucium flavum
YELLOW HORNED POPPY
☼ ✳✳✳   ↕ 60cm (24in) ↔ 45cm (18in)

Usually found on sand or shingle in the wild, this poppy bears bloomy blue-green leaves and stems, and yellow flowers in summer followed by narrow, curved fruits.

Kniphofia 'Atlanta'
RED HOT POKER
☼ ☼ ✳✳✳   ↕ 1.2m (4ft) ↔ 75cm (30in)

A magnificent evergreen, forming bold
clumps of strap-shaped, grey-green leaves.
Stout-stemmed orange-red pokers open to
yellow flowers in late spring and summer.

**OTHER PERENNIALS TOLERANT
OF COASTAL EXPOSURE**

Anthemis punctata subsp. *cupaniana*
Centranthus ruber, see p.86
Crambe cordifolia, see p.22
Dierama pulcherrimum, see p.22
Erigeron glaucus
Helichrysum italicum, see p.121
Nipponanthemum nipponicum
Othonna cheirifolia
Senecio cineraria 'White Diamond'
Yucca filamentosa

Pennisetum alopecuroides 'Hameln'
FOUNTAIN GRASS
☼ ✳✳   ↕ 1m (3ft) ↔ 1.4m (4½ft)

Borne in summer, the bottlebrush-like,
greenish white heads of spikelets, ageing
to grey- then golden brown, arch on long
stems over the elegant mounds of leaves.

Papaver orientale 'Cedric Morris'
ORIENTAL POPPY
☼ ✳✳✳   ↕ ↔ 90cm (36in)

An exquisite form of a cottage-garden
staple, forming bold clumps of hairy grey
leaves. Its large, frilly-margined, soft pink
blooms open from late spring to summer.

Platycodon grandiflorus
BALLOON FLOWER
☼ ☼ ✳✳✳✳   ↕ 60cm (24in) ↔ 30cm (12in)

The large, purple-blue bell-flowers open
from balloon-like, inflated buds during
late summer. Blue-green leaves clothe the
clumps of erect, branching stems.   ♉

Senecio cineraria 'Silver Dust'
SENECIO
☼ ✳✳✳   ↕ ↔ 30cm (12in)

Silver-grey felt covers the deeply divided
leaves and stems of this striking, woody-
based evergreen. Loose heads of mustard-
yellow flowers are borne in summer.   ♉

Perennials Tolerant of Exposure Inland

OTHER PERENNIALS TOLERANT
OF EXPOSURE INLAND

Achillea ptarmica 'Boule de Neige',
  see p.48
Alchemilla mollis, see p.84
Astilbe chinensis var. *pumila*
Cynoglossum nervosum
Geranium himalayense 'Gravetye'
Primula denticulata
Pulmonaria saccharata 'Mrs. Moon'
Senecio tanguticus, see p.118
Veronica gentianoides

EXPOSURE TO PERSISTENT or strong winds, particularly in cold areas, can severely damage or stunt the growth of garden plants. There is a surprisingly large variety of hardy perennials, however, that will grow, if not thrive, in such conditions, especially if they are given some form of shelter or protection from the worst of the elements.

Alchemilla conjuncta
LADY'S MANTLE
☼ ◑ ❄❄❄   ↕ 10cm (4in) ↔ 50cm (20in)

A tough, creeping perennial, providing excellent ground cover with its carpet of attractively fingered leaves, silvery-silky beneath. Green flowers open in summer.

Astrantia major 'Hadspen Blood'
MASTERWORT
☼ ◑ ❄❄❄   ↕ 45cm (18in) ↔ 60cm (24in)

Attractive enough with its clumps of long-stalked, deeply lobed and toothed leaves, this masterwort has the added bonus of loose heads of dark red flowers in summer.

Brunnera macrophylla
BRUNNERA
☼ ❄❄❄   ↕ 45cm (18in) ↔ 60cm (24in)

In spring, this tough, reliable perennial produces branched heads of bright blue, forget-me-not flowers above bold clumps of heart-shaped, softly-hairy leaves.   ♔

Anaphalis margaritacea
PEARLY EVERLASTING
☼ ❄❄❄   ↕ ↔ 60cm (24in)

The erect clumps of grey-woolly stems bear narrow leaves, white-woolly beneath, and dense clusters of papery, 'everlasting' flowerheads from summer to autumn.

Bergenia x *schmidtii*
ELEPHANT'S EAR
☼ ◑ ❄❄❄   ↕ 30cm (12in) ↔ 60cm (24in)

One of the most dependable perennials, reliably bearing large clusters of rose-pink flowers from late winter to spring, above mounds of leathery, rich green leaves.   ♔

Centaurea montana f. *alba*
PERENNIAL CORNFLOWER
☼ ❄❄❄   ↕ 45cm (18in) ↔ 60cm (24in)

This handsome form of the popular, blue-flowered perennial bears bold, pure white cornflowers above clumps of grey-green, leafy stems from late spring into summer.

Euphorbia polychroma
SPURGE
☀ ◑ ❄❄❄ ↕40cm (16in) ↔ 30cm (12in)

An invaluable and utterly reliable plant,
forming a rounded clump of leafy stems
which bear long-lasting, greenish yellow
flowerheads from spring into summer. ♔

Leucanthemum × superbum 'Wirral
Pride'
☀ ◑ ❄❄❄ ↕75cm (30in) ↔ 60cm (24in)

In summer, the dark green-leaved stems
of this bold, clump-forming perennial bear
solitary, large, double white daisy-heads
with yellowish anemone centres. ♔

Polemonium 'Lambrook Mauve'
JACOB'S LADDER
☀ ◑ ❄❄❄ ↕↔45cm (18in)

Erect, branching stems bear loose clusters
of lilac-blue bell-flowers among the
rounded clumps of deeply divided leaves
during late spring and early summer. ♔

Primula 'Wanda'
PRIMROSE
☀ ◑ ❄❄❄ ↕15cm (6in) ↔ 20cm (8in)

This long-established and reliable garden
primrose never fails to produce its dark
claret-red flowers, above clumps of toothy
leaves, for a long period in spring. ♔

Rhodiola rosea
ROSEROOT
☀ ❄❄❄ ↕↔20cm (8in)

Dense heads of tiny yellow flowers top
the low clump of fleshy, leafy, blue-green
bloomy stems in summer. It is ideal for a
rock garden, dry wall, or as edging.

Thermopsis rhombifolia
THERMOPSIS
☀ ◑ ❄❄❄ ↕↔90cm (36in)

In early summer, spires of lupin-like
yellow flowers rise above leaves divided
into threes. This creeping perennial forms
extensive patches, and can be invasive.

Low-allergen Perennials

FOR PEOPLE WHO SUFFER FROM ASTHMA, hayfever, or other allergies aggravated by air-borne pollen, gardening and gardens often have to be avoided at certain times of the year, especially during summer. Brushing or touching the foliage or flowers of certain plants can also cause or exacerbate some skin allergies. The following insect-pollinated perennials, however, can usually be relied upon to be non-allergenic, and will allow everyone to enjoy the garden all year round.

Campanula trachelium 'Bernice'
NETTLE-LEAVED BELLFLOWER
☼ ☀ ✻✻✻ ↕ 75cm (30in) ↔ 30cm (12in)

A beautiful perennial, forming clumps of erect stems with sharply toothed leaves, and axillary, double, violet-blue bell-flowers in summer. It may need support.

Ajuga reptans 'Catlin's Giant'
BUGLE
☼ ☀ ✻✻✻ ↕ 15cm (6in) ↔ indefinite

Excellent for ground cover, this bugle has large, brown-green, evergreen leaves that age to green. Dark blue flower spikes are borne in late spring and summer. ♛

Astilbe 'Irrlicht'
ASTILBE
☼ ☀ ✻✻✻ ↕ ↔ 50cm (20in)

In late spring and early summer, striking, erect plumes of tiny white flowers top this astilbe's clumps of much-divided, dark green leaves. It enjoys a moist soil.

Aquilegia chrysantha 'Yellow Queen'
COLUMBINE
☼ ☀ ✻✻✻ ↕ 90cm (36in) ↔ 60cm (24in)

The branched stems of this vigorous, erect perennial bear attractive, divided, ferny leaves, and slender-spurred, golden yellow flowers during late spring and summer.

Bergenia 'Bressingham White'
ELEPHANT'S EAR
☼ ☀ ✻✻✻ ↕ 45cm (18in) ↔ 60cm (24in)

During spring, fleshy, upright stems freely bear loose clusters of bell-shaped, pure white flowers above the robust clumps of large, leathery, evergreen leaves. ♛

Digitalis 'Glory of Roundway'
FOXGLOVE
☼ ☀ ✻✻✻ ↕ 90cm (36in) ↔ 30cm (12in)

This choice hybrid of *D. purpurea* and *D. lutea* has branched, narrow-leaved stems, and long racemes of funnel-shaped, pale yellow, pink-tinted flowers in summer.

Geranium psilostemon
ARMENIAN CRANESBILL
☼ ☀ ❋❋❋ ↕ 1.2m (4ft) ↔ 90cm (36in)

Fantastic in flower, this striking cranesbill sends up a mound of dense, leafy stems, which are covered throughout summer with bright magenta, black-eyed blooms.

Hosta 'Blue Blush'
PLANTAIN LILY
☼ ☀ ❋❋❋ ↕ 20cm (8in) ↔ 40cm (16in)

One of the most striking hostas, forming clumps of lance-shaped, strongly veined, blue-green leaves. It bears bell-shaped, lavender-blue flowers in summer.

Paeonia 'Duchesse de Nemours'
PEONY
☼ ☀ ❋❋❋ ↕ ↔ 80cm (32in)

The large, fragrant, double white flowers of this strong-growing peony have yellow-based inner petals. Flushed green in bud, the blooms open in early summer. ♈

Penstemon 'Andenken an Friedrich Hahn'
☼ ☀ ❋❋❋ ↕ 75cm (30in) ↔ 60cm (24in)

Also known as *P.* 'Garnet', this is probably the most reliable perennial penstemon. Its deep red flowers are produced on strong, leafy stems from midsummer onwards. ♈

Sidalcea 'Oberon'
CHECKERBLOOM
☼ ❋❋❋ ↕ 1.2m (4ft) ↔ 45cm (18in)

During summer, the clumps of erect, leafy stems bear loose racemes of clear rose-pink mallow-flowers. The stem leaves are deeply lobed, the basal ones less so.

Veronica spicata subsp. *incana*
SPIKED SPEEDWELL
☼ ❋❋❋ ↕ 60cm (24in) ↔ 45cm (18in)

The dense spikes of purple-blue flowers, borne throughout summer, are in striking contrast to the densely silver-hairy stems and mat of silvery foliage beneath.

OTHER LOW-ALLERGEN PERENNIALS

Allium 'Globemaster', see p.82
Aruncus dioicus, see p.18
Astilbe 'Snowdrift'
Dicentra spectabilis
Epimedium x *versicolor* 'Sulphureum'
Hemerocallis 'Golden Chimes'
Hosta 'Honeybells', see p.110
Iris sibirica
Polemonium 'Lambrook Mauve', see p.79

Viola cornuta
HORNED VIOLET
☼ ☀ ❋❋❋ ↕ 15cm (6in) ↔ 40cm (16in)

An excellent and reliable small perennial with a low-spreading, slightly bushy habit and lightly scented, lilac-blue to violet flowers in late spring and summer. ♈

Slug-proof Perennials

SLUGS AND SNAILS UNDOUBTEDLY have a voracious appetite when they discover a tasty plant, but what they devour in one garden they will often only nibble at in another. Some plants, such as many hostas, are always a gourmet meal for slugs and snails and are readily consumed. Others, especially those with hard-textured, hairy, or poisonous leaves, are often relatively ignored. Here is a selection of the most reliably slug- and snail-proof perennials for the garden.

Bergenia 'Silberlicht'
ELEPHANT'S EAR
☼ ☼ ✳✳✳ ↕40cm (12in) ↔ 30cm (12in)

Fleshy, shining, evergreen leaves form a basal mound above which, in spring, rise erect, fleshy stems bearing loose clusters of white flowers that age to pink. ♔

Corydalis lutea
YELLOW CORYDALIS
☼ ☼ ✳✳✳ ↕35cm (14in) ↔ 30cm (12in)

The mound of ferny, evergreen leaves is used by snails as a refuge but rarely eaten. Slender racemes of tubular yellow flowers are borne from late spring to early autumn.

Allium 'Globemaster'
ORNAMENTAL ONION
☼ ✳✳✳ ↕80cm (32in) ↔ 30cm (12in)

Magnificent for group plantings, this bulb has arching, strap-shaped leaves, and huge spangled heads of deep violet flowers in summer. Loved by butterflies and bees.

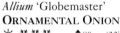

OTHER SLUG-PROOF PERENNIALS
Aconitum carmichaelii 'Arendsii', see p.96
Artemisia ludoviciana
Arum italicum 'Marmoratum', see p.135
Campanula persicifolia
Colchicum 'Waterlily', see p.96
Epimedium pinnatum subsp. *colchicum*, see p.46
Helleborus foetidus
Lobelia siphilitica
Sedum 'Matrona', see p.133

Aster ericoides 'Esther'
MICHAELMAS DAISY
☼ ✳✳✳ ↕70cm (28in) ↔ 30cm (12in)

Bushy clumps of leafy, slender-branched stems are topped by broad heads of small pink, yellow-eyed daisies in late summer and autumn. Useful for its late flowering.

Galanthus 'Atkinsii'
SNOWDROP
☼ ✳✳✳ ↕20cm (8in) ↔ 8cm (3in)

Ideal for naturalizing, this strong-growing bulb has narrow, fleshy, blue-green leaves. In late winter, erect stems bear pendent white flowers with green markings. ♔

Specific Uses

Geranium macrorrhizum
CRANESBILL
☼ ☀ ❄❄❄ ↕ 50cm (20in) ↔ 60cm (24in)

An adaptable and reliable, semi-evergreen carpeter, with lobed, aromatic leaves often colouring well in autumn. Clusters of pink to purple flowers appear in early summer.

Helleborus × *nigercors*
HELLEBORE
☼ ❄❄❄ ↕ 30cm (12in) ↔ 90cm (36in)

Welcome clusters of saucer-shaped, white or pink-tinted flowers open from winter to spring above the basal clump of divided, coarse-toothed, evergreen leaves. ▽

Hosta 'Halcyon'
PLANTAIN LILY
☼ ☀ ❄❄❄ ↕ ↔ 70cm (28in)

One of the best slug-proof hostas, forming bold clumps of attractive, heart-shaped, bluish grey leaves. It produces pendent, blue-grey bell-flowers during summer. ▽

Iris chrysographes
IRIS
☼ ❄❄❄ ↕ ↔ 50cm (20in)

One of my favourite species, this iris forms erect clumps of sword-shaped, grey-green leaves, with stems of fragrant, velvety, reddish purple flowers borne in summer.

Pulmonaria angustifolia subsp. *azurea*
PULMONARIA
☼ ☀ ❄❄❄ ↕ 25cm (10in) ↔ 45cm (18in)

A nice change from spotted varieties, with its low clump of rough-hairy green leaves. In spring, it bears nodding clusters of rich gentian-blue, tubular flowers, red in bud.

Rudbeckia hirta
BLACK-EYED SUSAN
☼ ☀ ❄❄❄ ↕ 80cm (30in) ↔ 90cm (36in)

If kept moist in summer, this cheery plant will bear a succession of dark-eyed, rich yellow daisies, good for cutting, from mid-summer to autumn.

Sedum spectabile 'Iceberg'
ICE PLANT
☼ ❄❄❄ ↕ ↔ 45cm (18in)

Reliable and easy to grow, with mounds of grey-green leaves and fleshy stems topped by flattened heads of white flowers from summer to autumn. Loved by butterflies.

Rabbit-proof Perennials

IT IS PROBABLY TRUE to say that rabbits are the most serious source of plant damage and loss in the garden, especially in country areas or those close to large, open spaces. Rabbits can eat their way through a bed or border faster than any slug or snail, and although various methods are recommended for their control, it does no harm to include some perennials in the garden that rabbits usually find unpalatable or uninteresting.

Agapanthus 'Blue Giant'
AFRICAN LILY

☼ ✳✳✳   ↕ 90cm (36in) ↔ 60cm (24in)

In late summer and early autumn, stout stems bearing large, loose heads of rich blue flowers rise above the bold clump of long, strap-shaped green leaves.

Alchemilla mollis
LADY'S MANTLE

☼ ◐ ✳✳✳   ↕ ↔ 35cm (14in)

This adaptable, reliable plant has mounds of downy, scalloped and lobed, grey-green leaves, topped by yellowish green flower clusters in summer. Will seed around. ♔

Aster ericoides 'Golden Spray'
ASTER

☼ ✳✳✳   ↕ 90cm (36in) ↔ 30cm (12in)

From late summer into autumn, branched heads of small white, pink-tinted daisies, with rich yellow centres, are produced on a bushy clump of erect, leafy stems. ♔

Astilbe 'Straussenfeder'
ASTILBE

☼ ◐ ✳✳✳   ↕ 90cm (36in) ↔ 60cm (24in)

Known also as 'Ostrich Plume', which neatly describes its arching sprays of pink flowers in summer and autumn. Young leaves are attractively bronze-tinted. ♔

Bergenia stracheyi
ELEPHANT'S EAR

☼ ✳✳✳   ↕ 20cm (8in) ↔ 30cm (12in)

The low mound of leathery, evergreen leaves is crowned in early spring by dense clusters of fragrant pink bell-flowers. It is excellent for ground cover or path edging.

Euphorbia griffithii 'Fireglow'
SPURGE

☼ ◐ ✳✳✳   ↕ 75cm (30in) ↔ 90cm (36in)

A vigorous, creeping perennial, eventually forming large patches of leafy stems that colour richly in autumn. Terminal clusters of fiery orange flowers open in summer.

Helleborus × *hybridus*
LENTEN ROSE

◐ ✳✳✳   ↕ ↔ 45cm (18in)

A beautiful and sought-after group of hybrids, bearing semi-evergreen leaves and large, nodding, saucer-shaped flowers in a range of colours from late winter to spring.

Lamium maculatum 'Beacon Silver'
DEAD NETTLE
☼ ☼ ❄❄❄   ↕ 20cm (8in) ↔ 1m (3ft)

Extensive carpets of toothed, silvery,
green-margined leaves provide excellent,
semi-evergreen ground cover. Clusters of
pale pink flowers are borne in summer.

OTHER RABBIT-PROOF PERENNIALS
Aconitum 'Blue Sceptre'
Anemone x *hybrida* 'Königin Charlotte', see p.50
Aquilegia 'Magpie'
Aster novi-belgii 'Marie Ballard'
Convallaria majalis 'Fortin's Giant'
Crocosmia 'Lucifer'
Kniphofia triangularis, see p.105
Nepeta nervosa
Pulmonaria saccharata
Sedum 'Matrona', see p.133

Paeonia officinalis 'Rubra Plena'
PEONY
☼ ☼ ❄❄❄   ↕ 75cm (30in) ↔ 90cm (36in)

The reliable, old-fashioned, double red
peony of cottage gardens. It forms clumps
of glossy green leaves, and bears crimson
blooms with ruffled petals in summer. ♔

Narcissus 'Mount Hood'
DAFFODIL
☼ ☼ ❄❄❄   ↕ 45cm (18in) ↔ 50cm (20in)

A classic large-flowered trumpet daffodil,
producing gorgeous white flowers with
cream-coloured trumpets in spring. It is
superb when planted in groups.

Trollius x *cultorum* 'Earliest of All'
GLOBEFLOWER
☼ ☼ ❄❄❄   ↕ 50cm (20in) ↔ 40cm (16in)

Not the first, but still an early perennial,
forming loose clumps of deep-cut leaves.
Branched stems bear globular, clear yellow
flowers in spring. Prefers heavy soils.

Veratrum album
FALSE HELLEBORE
☼ ☼ ❄❄❄   ↕ 2m (6ft) ↔ 60cm (24in)

Worth growing for its large, handsomely
pleated leaves alone, this bold perennial is
impressive in groups. The tall plumes of
white flowers in summer are a bonus.

Deer-proof Perennials

AFTER RABBITS AND HARES, the most destructive garden visitors are deer, although, like rabbits, they are mainly a problem for gardeners in rural and wooded areas. It can be disheartening to find favourite plants repeatedly demolished by browsing deer, but providing deterrents or erecting fences is often impractical and expensive. One effective alternative, however, is to grow at least some perennials that deer are known to find uninteresting or, better still, unpalatable.

Centranthus ruber
RED VALERIAN
☼ ❄❄❄   ↕ 90cm (36in) ↔ 60cm (24in)

Often found on old walls, this woody-based perennial has bold clumps of leafy, grey-green stems, and fragrant, pink, red, or white flowers. It thrives in alkaline soil.

Aconitum lycoctonum subsp. *vulparia*
WOLFSBANE
☼ ◑ ❄❄❄   ↕ 1.5m (5ft) ↔ 90cm (36in)

This handsome perennial has finely cut, glossy green leaves and produces straw-yellow flowers in summer. Its roots were once used in parts of Europe as wolf bait.

Astilbe 'Deutschland'
ASTILBE
☼ ◑ ❄❄❄   ↕ 50cm (20in) ↔ 30cm (12in)

In summer, erect panicles of white flowers top the bright, glossy green mound of deeply divided leaves. Good for cutting, it needs some moisture in summer to excel.

Artemisia ludoviciana 'Silver Queen'
ARTEMISIA
☼ ❄❄❄   ↕↔ 75cm (30in)

A clump-forming but creeping perennial, worth growing for its lance-shaped, silver-white leaves, and white-woolly flower-heads borne from summer onwards. ⏚

OTHER DEER-PROOF PERENNIALS

Aconitum napellus 'Carneum'
Allium schoenoprasum 'Forescate',
   see p.48
Asplenium scolopendrium, see p.140
Aster novi-belgii 'Royal Velvet'
Bergenia 'Ballawley', see p.135
Epimedium perralderianum, see p.34
Geranium sanguineum
Helleborus × hybridus, see p.84
Iris foetidissima
Kniphofia uvaria
Lamium maculatum 'White Nancy'
Paeonia 'Bowl of Beauty'
Rudbeckia fulgida var. *sullivantii*
   'Goldsturm', see p.17
Sisyrinchium striatum
Tellima grandiflora, see p.115
Trollius × cultorum 'Earliest of All',
   see p.85

Digitalis purpurea Excelsior Hybrids
FOXGLOVE
☼ ❄❄❄   ↕ 2m (6ft) ↔ 60cm (24in)

A bold and colourful, short-lived perennial or biennial, with a rosette of hairy leaves, and a tall spire of funnel-shaped flowers in pastel shades in early summer. ⏚

Narcissus 'Spellbinder'
DAFFODIL
☼ ☀ ❄❄❄   ↕↔ 50cm (20in)

A strong-growing daffodil, especially
impressive when planted in bold drifts.
The spring flowers are sulphur-yellow,
with coronas fading to white with age. ♆

Geranium macrorrhizum 'Bevan's
Variety'
☼ ☀ ❄❄❄   ↕ 50cm (20in) ↔ 60cm (24in)

An excellent, all-round, semi-evergreen
plant, especially useful as ground cover. It
flowers in early summer, and has aromatic
leaves that often colour well in autumn.

Papaver orientale 'Beauty of
Livermere'
☼ ❄❄❄   ↕↔ 90cm (36in)

From late spring into summer, erect, hairy
stems bear pale salmon-pink flowers, with
basal black blotches, above a bold clump
of deeply cut, hairy leaves. ♆

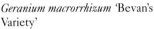

Iris orientalis
IRIS
☼ ❄❄❄   ↕↔ 90cm (36in)

This robust perennial forms erect clumps
or patches of strap-shaped leaves. In early
summer, stiff stems carry a succession of
white, yellow-stained flowers.

Lysimachia clethroides
LOOSESTRIFE
☼ ☀ ❄❄❄   ↕ 90cm (36in) ↔ 60cm (24in)

A vigorous perennial once established,
forming a clump of erect, narrowly leafy
stems. Its characteristic swan-neck spikes
of white flowers are borne in summer. ♆

x *Solidaster luteus* 'Lemore'
HYBRID GOLDEN ROD
☼ ❄❄❄   ↕↔ 80cm (32in)

The dense clumps of erect stems, clothed
in narrow leaves, sport sparsely branched
heads of pale lemon-yellow flowers from
summer to autumn. Good for cutting. ♆

Floral Effect

FLOWERS ARE THE GREATEST ATTRIBUTE of many perennials, and can be relied upon to bring colour and fragrance to any garden or home. With blooms in all shades and shapes, in some cases produced over several months, there is scope for imaginative combinations, and for flowers all year round.

△ SUMMER BLOOMS *Mixed colours and flower forms are the strength of this scree planting, which flanks an informal path.*

Anemone hupehensis 'September Charm' for autumn flowers

Whatever their other attractions, most gardeners grow perennials for their often abundant and reliably borne flowers. In all but the coldest areas, where snow or ice lie heavy on the garden during winter, there is hardly a day in the year when a perennial of some kind is not flowering. From spring to summer, and on into autumn, perennials can provide gardens with an unbroken, colourful and fragrant display. Even in winter, there is a small but reliable fraternity of perennials that flowers despite the often poor light and intimidating cold.

FLOWER COLOUR

With flowers ranging from white and subtle pastel shades to strident reds and golden yellows, perennials will bring a truly formidable range of colours to the garden. These colours can be used to create varied effects, depending on whether you choose to mix them in a natural arrangement, or match them as part of a more structured theme. The strong colour contrasts often seen in the wild, where perennials such as golden rod (*Solidago*) and blue michaelmas daisies (*Aster*) grow together, can also be used to inspire plantings in the garden – or even recreated using the same or similar plants. Alternatively, a selection of plants with similarly toned blooms, whether hot, cool, or pale in colour, can be grown together to evoke a particular mood. For a more formal design, themed borders using only one flower colour are also an option.

FORM AND STRUCTURE

Flowerheads make an important, if temporary, contribution to the form and structure of a garden landscape. Varying from the statuesque to the fragile, the spheres, plumes, sprays, tall spikes, or flattened flowerheads of perennials can be combined for eye-catching contrast and effect.

△ HOT COLOURS *A fiery display of* Hemerocallis *'Stafford' and* Lilium *'Enchantment' brings warmth to a border.*

◁ STRONG CONTRAST *Striking effects can be achieved by using a few contrasting colours, here mainly blue and yellow.*

▷ INFORMAL BEAUTY *Pale oriental poppies, foxgloves, and* Dictamnus *make a delightful study in height and colour.*

Perennials with Spring Flowers

NO GARDEN PERENNIALS are more eagerly awaited than those that flower in spring. This is especially true in cold climates, where there is often little colour in the garden to relieve the long, bleak winters. With the increasing warmth and daylight of spring, the garden is rejuvenated as a wealth of perennials, including many bulbs, burst into flower.

Bergenia 'Sunningdale'
ELEPHANT'S EAR
☼ ☀ ❄❄❄ ‡ 45cm (18in) ↔ 60cm (24in)

The evergreen, rounded, leathery leaves turn a warm copper-red in winter. Spring brings loose clusters of bell-shaped, lilac-magenta flowers on fleshy red stems.

Chionodoxa luciliae
SNOW GLORY
☼ ❄❄❄ ‡ 15cm (6in) ↔ 10cm (4in)

One of the loveliest and most reliable of early spring bulbs, with loose clusters of starry, sky-blue, white-eyed flowers. It is impressive planted in groups or drifts. ♔

Hylomecon japonica
HYLOMECON
☼ ☀ ❄❄❄ ‡ ↔ 30cm (12in)

This charming poppy relative is excellent in woodland, especially as a ground cover. It has deeply divided, toothed leaves and bears its simple flowers into early summer.

OTHER EVERGREEN PERENNIALS WITH SPRING FLOWERS

Aurinia saxatilis
Bergenia × *schmidtii*, see p.78
Epimedium pinnatum subsp. *colchicum*, see p.46
Erysimum 'Bowles' Mauve'
Euphorbia characias subsp. *wulfenii* 'Lambrook Gold'
Helleborus argutifolius, see p.114
Helleborus foetidus
Iberis sempervirens

Boykinia jamesii
BOYKINIA
☼ ❄❄❄ PH ‡ ↔ 15cm (6in)

A choice perennial, bearing loose sprays of frilled, pinkish red, green-centred bell-flowers above its hummocks of rounded or kidney-shaped, glandular-hairy leaves. ♔

Doronicum orientale 'Frühlingspracht'
DORONICUM
☼ ☀ ❄❄❄ ‡ 40cm (16in) ↔ 90cm (36in)

Its German name, 'Spring Beauty', aptly describes this colourful perennial, with its double, golden yellow flowerheads above clumps of heart-shaped, scalloped leaves.

Lathyrus vernus 'Alboroseus'
SPRING VETCHLING
☼ ☀ ❄❄❄ ‡ 40cm (16in) ↔ 45cm (18in)

The crowded, erect stems of this reliable clump-former bear deeply divided leaves and loose, one-sided racemes of pink and white pea-flowers. Excellent with bulbs.

Primula denticulata var. *alba*
DRUMSTICK PRIMULA
☼ ☀ ✳✳✳ ↕ ↔ 45cm (18in)

This is the white form of a popular and easily grown perennial. Its rounded heads of yellow-eyed flowers are carried on stout stems above leafy foliage rosettes.

Leucojum vernum var. *carpathicum*
SPRING SNOWFLAKE
☼ ☀ ✳✳✳ ↕ 25cm (10in) ↔ 15cm (6in)

Charming for group plantings, this bulb forms tufts of strap-shaped, fleshy leaves. Erect, fleshy stems bear nodding white bell-flowers with yellow-tipped segments.

Pulmonaria 'Mawson's Blue'
PULMONARIA
☼ ☀ ✳✳✳ ↕ 35cm (14in) ↔ 45cm (18in)

Low clumps of softly-hairy leaves and clusters of dark blue flowers appear from late winter to spring. A pretty alternative to pulmonarias with spotted leaves.

OTHER HERBACEOUS PERENNIALS WITH SPRING FLOWERS

Adonis vernalis, see p.98
Bergenia ciliata
Brunnera macrophylla, see p.78
Cardamine heptaphylla
Euphorbia polychroma, see p.79
Hacquetia epipactis, see p.37
Helleborus × *hybridus*, see p.84
Pachyphragma macrophyllum
Trollius × *cultorum* 'Earliest of All', see p.85

Narcissus 'King Alfred'
DAFFODIL
☼ ☀ ✳✳✳ ↕ 45cm (18in) ↔ 30cm (12in)

Spectacular in large groups or drifts, this long-established daffodil is very popular for naturalizing. The large, golden yellow trumpet-flowers open on strong stems.

Narcissus 'Thalia'
DAFFODIL
☼ ☀ ✳✳✳ ↕ 35cm (14in) ↔ 15cm (6in)

One of a group of hybrids of *N. triandrus*, this beautiful daffodil has upright stems, each carrying a pair of nodding, milk-white flowers with yellow-tinged throats.

Perennials with Flowers from Early to Midsummer

AFTER THE INITIAL RUSH OF FLOWERS during spring, the scene is set for the countless perennials that flower from early to midsummer or, in some cases, beyond. They include many of our most popular and reliable garden plants, as well as others perhaps less well known though equally desirable, and provide us with the first blooms for summer borders.

FLORAL EFFECT

Buphthalmum salicifolium
BUPHTHALMUM
☼ ☼ ❄❄❄ ↕ 60cm (24in) ↔ 45cm (18in)

Yellow daisy-flowers, excellent for cutting, are borne continuously during summer. The clumps of erect stems are clothed in narrow, willow-like, dark geen leaves.

Aconitum 'Ivorine'
MONKSHOOD
☼ ☼ ❄❄❄ ↕↔ 90cm (36in)

A vigorous, bushy perennial with deeply lobed, jaggedly cut leaves. In late spring and early summer, branching stems carry dense racemes of hooded ivory flowers.

SMALL PERENNIALS WITH EARLY/ MIDSUMMER BLOOMS

Amsonia orientalis
Anthericum liliago, see p.30
Centaurea hypoleuca 'John Coutts', see p.76
Digitalis grandiflora
Geranium endressii
Hemerocallis 'Golden Chimes'
Incarvillea delavayi, see p.118
Paradisea liliastrum
Polemonium carneum

Delphinium 'Fanfare'
DELPHINIUM
☼ ❄❄❄ ↕ 2.2m (7ft) ↔ 45cm (18in)

Tall and beautiful, this impressive plant has deeply cut, lobed leaves, and dense, branched racemes of semi-double, white-eyed, silver-mauve summer flowers. ⚜

Baptisia australis
FALSE INDIGO
☼ ❄❄❄ ↕ 1.5m (5ft) ↔ 90cm (36in)

The long racemes of blue, white-marked pea-flowers in early summer are followed by inflated seed pods. Stems and three-parted leaves are a bloomy blue-green. ⚜

Geranium 'Johnson's Blue'
CRANESBILL
☼ ☀ ❄❄❄ ↕45cm (18in) ↔60cm (24in)

One of the best garden cranesbills, this forms a clump of long-stalked, deep-cut leaves and freely bears lavender-blue summer flowers with paler eyes. ♔

Iris 'Blue-eyed Brunette'
BEARDED IRIS
☼ ☀ ❄❄❄ ↕90cm (36in) ↔60cm (24in)

The typical fans of sword-shaped, grey-green leaves are topped, in early summer, by striking, large, reddish brown flowers with lilac splashes and golden beards. ♔

Scabiosa caucasica 'Clive Greaves'
SCABIOUS
☼ ❄❄❄ ↕↔60cm (24in)

This long-established favourite is always reliable in its flowering. The flattened, lavender-blue flowerheads, excellent for cutting, are borne over a long period. ♔

Gypsophila paniculata 'Bristol Fairy'
☼ ❄❄❄ ↕↔1.1m (3½ft)

A favourite with florists, this popular perennial produces a loose mound of slender, branching stems and clouds of small, double white summer flowers. ♔

MEDIUM TO TALL PERENNIALS WITH EARLY/MIDSUMMER BLOOMS

Aruncus dioicus, see p.18
Cimicifuga racemosa
Crambe cordifolia, see p.22
Euphorbia griffithii 'Fireglow', see p.84
Geranium psilostemon, see p.81
Iris sibirica
Macleaya microcarpa 'Kelway's Coral Plume'
Papaver orientale 'Cedric Morris', see p.77

Hemerocallis middendorffii
DAYLILY
☼ ❄❄❄ ↕90cm (36in) ↔45cm (18in)

In early summer, the star-shaped, fragrant, orange-yellow flowers open from reddish brown buds over a bold clump of arching, semi-evergreen, strap-shaped leaves.

Malva alcea var. *fastigiata*
MALLOW
☼ ❄❄❄ ↕80cm (32in) ↔60cm (24in)

The continuous display of large, five-petalled, deep pink mallow-flowers often lasts into autumn. Finely divided leaves clothe the narrow clumps of erect stems.

Stachys macrantha
STACHYS
☼ ❄❄❄ ↕60cm (24in) ↔30cm (12in)

From early summer onwards, the already attractive rosettes of wrinkly, scalloped, heart-shaped leaves are joined by spikes of long-tubed, pink-purple flowers.

FLORAL EFFECT

93

Perennials with Flowers from Mid- to Late Summer

MANY OF THE PERENNIALS that flower in the middle of summer do so over a long period, taking advantage of the available warmth and sunlight. The following selection includes some plants that begin flowering in early summer, and others that continue blooming into early autumn, earning their place in the garden by extending the period of interest.

Inula ensifolia
INULA
☼ ☀ ✳✳✳ ↕60cm (24in) ↔30cm (12in)

A thoroughly reliable plant with narrow leaves and dense, bushy clumps of erect stems. These carry golden yellow daisy-heads continuously over a long period.

Aster amellus 'Veilchenkönigin'
ASTER
☼ ✳✳✳ ↕50cm (20in) ↔45cm (18in)

An excellent late summer perennial with clumps of erect, leafy stems topped by broad, flattened heads of yellow-centred, violet-purple daisy-flowers. ♔

Kniphofia 'Samuel's Sensation'
TORCH LILY
☼ ☀ ✳✳✳ ↕1.5m (5ft) ↔75cm (30in)

From late summer to early autumn, the bold clumps of long, strap-shaped leaves are dwarfed by stiff-stemmed heads of bright scarlet flowers, ageing to yellow. ♔

OTHER PERENNIALS WITH FLOWERS IN MIDSUMMER

Campanula latifolia var. *macrantha*
Centranthus ruber, see p.86
Crocosmia 'Lucifer'
Galega 'His Majesty'
Hemerocallis 'Stafford'
Macleaya cordata
Prunella grandiflora
Stachys macrantha
Veronica austriaca subsp. *teucrium* 'Crater Lake Blue'

Coreopsis grandiflora 'Badengold'
TICKSEED
☼ ☀ ✳✳✳ ↕90cm (36in) ↔45cm (18in)

This bright, cheerful-looking perennial has finely divided leaves and clumps of erect stems bearing orange-centred, deep yellow daisies throughout summer.

Digitalis x *mertonensis*
FOXGLOVE
☼ ☀ ✳✳✳ ↕90cm (36in) ↔30cm (12in)

"Crushed strawberry" exactly describes the colour of the tubular summer flowers of this robust, clump-forming plant. Its veiny leaves are also attractive. ♔

Lavatera 'Rosea'
MALLOW
☼ ❄❄   ↕ ↔ 2m (6ft)

Easily one of the most popular and
reliable mallows, forming a large, woody-
based, semi-evergreen bush, covered with
deep pink flowers during summer. 🏆

**OTHER PERENNIALS WITH
FLOWERS IN LATE SUMMER**

Aconitum 'Bressingham Spire'
Anemone x *hybrida* 'Königin Charlotte',
  see p.50
Aster cordifolius 'Sweet Lavender'
Gentiana asclepiadea, see p.107
Helenium 'Septemberfuchs', see p.104

Nepeta sibirica
NEPETA
☼ ☼ ❄❄❄   ↕ 90cm (36in) ↔ 45cm (18in)

Aromatic, toothy leaves clothe the erect
clumps of four-angled stems. The long,
interrupted spikes of large, deep violet to
lilac-blue flowers are loved by bees.

Salvia x *sylvestris*
'Mainacht'
☼ ❄❄❄   ↕ 60cm (24in) ↔ 30cm (12in)

Its German name, 'May Night', aptly
describes the velvety, dark indigo-blue
flowers, with purple bracts, borne in long
spikes on leafy, four-angled stems. 🏆

Monarda 'Prärienacht'
BERGAMOT
☼ ☼ ❄❄❄❄   ↕ 90cm (36in) ↔ 60cm (24in)

The dense clumps of downy, four-angled
stems bear crowded heads of purple-lilac
flowers with red-tinted green bracts. All
parts are aromatic when bruised.

Physostegia virginiana 'Vivid'
OBEDIENT PLANT
☼ ☼ ❄❄❄❄   ↕ 60m (24in) ↔ 30cm (12in)

During summer, spikes of bright purple-
pink flowers, excellent for cutting, top
the dense clumps of four-angled, smooth,
erect stems, clothed in narrow leaves. 🏆

Verbena bonariensis
VERBENA
☼ ❄❄   ↕ 2m (6ft) ↔ 45cm (18in)

Bees, butterflies, and hoverflies are all
attracted to the delicate clusters of tiny,
lilac-purple flowers that crown the tall,
branching stems. It will seed freely.

FLORAL EFFECT

Perennials with Autumn Flowers

FOR MANY GARDENERS, especially in cool-temperate zones, autumn is dominated by the brilliant tints of dying leaves and the equally colourful effect of seed heads, berries, and other fruits. Comparatively few perennials choose to flower at this time, but those that do are all the more valued, as their late displays enliven the garden before the onset of winter.

Cyclamen hederifolium
DWARF CYCLAMEN
☀ ❄❄❄ ↕ 10cm (4in) ↔ 15cm (6in)

Neatly lobed, beautifully marbled leaves follow the exquisite, slender-stalked, pink or white flowers. Useful for ground cover under trees or for group plantings. ♔

Aconitum carmichaelii 'Arendsii'
MONKSHOOD
☀ ☀ ❄❄❄ ↕ 1.2m (4ft) ↔ 60cm (24in)

A bold, clump-forming perennial valued for its stems of dense, deeply cut, dark green leaves and panicles of helmeted, purple-blue, dark-eyed flowers.

Cimicifuga simplex 'Elstead'
BUGBANE
☀ ❄❄❄ ↕ 1.2m (4ft) ↔ 60cm (24in)

The tall, arching stems of this graceful perennial bear long, cylindrical racemes of tiny white flowers above deeply divided, dark green to purple-tinted leaves. ♔

Leucanthemella serotina
MOON DAISY
☀ ☀ ❄❄❄ ↕ 2m (6ft) ↔ 90cm (36in)

Late and lovely, this bold daisy has clumps of tall, leafy stems and sprays of big white blooms that face and follow the sun. Once known as *Chrysanthemum uliginosum*. ♔

Anemone hupehensis 'September Charm'
JAPANESE ANEMONE
☀ ☀ ❄❄❄ ↕ 75cm (30in) ↔ 60cm (24in)

All the so-called Japanese anemones are reliable and useful. This one forms clumps of dark shoots with three-lobed leaflets and a long succession of clear pink flowers. ♔

Colchicum 'Waterlily'
AUTUMN CROCUS
☀ ❄❄❄ ↕ 12cm (5in) ↔ 10cm (4in)

This is one of the most spectacular dwarf bulbs, especially in large drifts. Its double, slender-tubed, pinkish lilac blooms may need support. Leaves emerge in spring.

Nerine bowdenii 'Mark Fenwick'
NERINE
☀ ❄❄❄ ↕ 45cm (18in) ↔ 30cm (12in)

Spectacular in autumn, this bulb's smooth stems flaunt loose umbels of lily-like pink flowers. The broad, strap-shaped leaves follow later. It is superb in group plantings.

Schizostylis coccinea 'Major'
KAFFIR LILY
☼ ❄❄ ↕ 60cm (24in) ↔ 30cm (12in)

This member of the *Gladiolus* family bears
flattened, sword-shaped leaves and bold
spikes of large, satiny red flowers. Plant it
in groups for a striking effect. ▽

**OTHER PERENNIALS WITH
AUTUMN FLOWERS**

Aster cordifolius 'Sweet Lavender'
Colchicum speciosum 'Album'
Eupatorium purpureum
  'Atropurpureum', see p.18
Kniphofia triangularis, see p.105
Leucojum autumnale
Sedum 'Carmen'
Senecio tanguticus, see p.118
Tricyrtis hirta var. *alba*
Verbena bonariensis, see p.95

Strobilanthes atropurpureus
STROBILANTHES
☼ ☀ ❄❄❄ ↕ 1.2m (4ft) ↔ 90cm (36in)

Not commonly grown but an excellent
perennial, freely bearing curved, hooded,
indigo-blue or purple flowers on densely
branched, bushy, and leafy stems.

Sedum 'Vera Jameson'
STONECROP
☼ ❄❄❄ ↕ 25cm (10in) ↔ 45cm (18in)

A true gem among the autumn-flowering
sedums, this has low hummocks of pink-
purple, bloomy leaves and crowded heads
of star-shaped, rose-pink flowers. ▽

Tricyrtis formosana
TOAD LILY
☼ ☀ ❄❄❄ ↕ 80cm (32in) ↔ 45cm (18in)

The curious white, red-purple-spotted
flowers of this erect, clump-forming plant
deserve a close look to fully appreciate
their beauty. The foliage is handsome too.

Vernonia crinita
VERNONIA
☼ ☀ ❄❄❄ ↕ 2m (6ft) ↔ 90cm (3ft)

From late summer to autumn, flattened
clusters of reddish purple flowerheads top
the erect, strong-growing, narrow-leaved
stems of this stately vernonia.

Perennials with Winter Flowers

I N COOL-TEMPERATE CLIMATES, where winter brings most growth to a standstill, the appearance of any plant in flower is always a surprise. However, certain perennials, including many bulbs, bloom in winter despite the hostile conditions. Those suggested here will provide interest at a time when other herbaceous plants have died down or lost their leaves.

FLORAL EFFECT

Eranthis hyemalis
WINTER ACONITE
☀ ☀ ✻✻✻   ↕ 8cm (3in) ↔ 5cm (2in)

Plant this aconite in quantity to encourage large drifts. Its cup-shaped, bright yellow flowers are a cheery sight above the ruffs of toothed leaves in winter and spring. ▽

> **OTHER PERENNIALS WITH WINTER FLOWERS**
>
> *Adonis amurensis*
> *Bergenia* x *schmidtii*, see p.78
> *Eranthis* x *tubergenii* 'Guinea Gold'
> *Galanthus nivalis* 'Flore Pleno'
> *Helleborus argutifolius*, see p.114
> *Helleborus* x *sternii* Blackthorn Group
> *Narcissus* 'Rijnveld's Early Sensation'
> *Pulmonaria rubra* 'Redstart'
> *Petasites fragrans*
> *Viola odorata*

Adonis vernalis
ADONIS
☀ ✻✻✻   ↕ 38cm (15in) ↔ 45cm (18in)

In late winter and spring, cupped, golden yellow flowers top the clumps of deeply divided, ferny, bright green leaves. It will flower earlier in containers or if sheltered.

Crocus tommasinianus
CROCUS
☀ ☀ ✻✻✻   ↕ 10cm (4in) ↔ 7.5cm (3in)

Easily naturalized, this popular bulb bears slender-tubed, scented, pale silvery lilac to reddish purple flowers from winter to early spring, above narrow leaves. ▽

Arisarum vulgare
MONK'S COWL
☀ ☀ ✻✻✻   ↕ 15cm (6in) ↔ 13cm (5in)

This curious *Arum* relative bears broadly arrow-shaped green leaves, followed by hooded, brown- or purple-striped flowers, each with a protruding "nose".

Cyclamen coum f. *albissimum*
HARDY CYCLAMEN
☀ ☀ ✻✻✻   ↕ 10cm (4in) ↔ 15cm (6in)

The low hummocks of kidney-shaped, fleshy green or attractively marbled leaves are accompanied in winter by small white flowers with carmine-red mouths.

Galanthus nivalis 'Sandersii'
SNOWDROP
☀ ✻✻✻   ↕ ↔ 10cm (4in)

A charming and unusual variation of the familiar snowdrop, in which the flower ovaries and the tips of the inner segments are bright yellow. It is slow to increase.

Iris unguicularis 'Walter Butt'
IRIS

☼ ❄❄❄ ↕30cm (12in) ↔40cm (16in)

Over many weeks, this beautiful winter-flowerer produces a succession of large, fragrant, pale lavender-blue flowers from clumps of narrow, evergreen leaves.

Galanthus reginae-olgae subsp. *vernalis*
SNOWDROP

☼ ❄❄❄ ↕↔10cm (4in)

Borne in late winter and spring, the faintly scented, nodding white flowers have inner segments tipped green. It differs from the common snowdrop in its darker leaves.

Lathraea clandestina
BLUE TOOTHWORT

☼ ☼ ❄❄❄❄ ↕5cm (2in) ↔30cm (12in)

This parasitic plant can grow on the roots of trees such as alder, willow, and poplar. Two-lipped mauve flowers emerge from the white, scaly clumps during late winter.

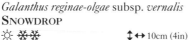

Helleborus foetidus 'Wester Flisk'
STINKING HELLEBORE

☼ ☼ ❄❄❄❄ ↕80cm (32in) ↔45cm (18in)

The stems, finger-like leaves, and flower-stalks of this outstanding, evergreen plant are suffused with red. The pendent, pale green bell-flowers have purple mouths.

Helleborus niger 'Potter's Wheel'
CHRISTMAS ROSE

☼ ❄❄❄❄ ↕30cm (12in) ↔45cm (18in)

A reliable selection of a favourite cottage-garden perennial, producing bowl-shaped white flowers, with green eyes, above low clumps of leathery, overwintering foliage.

Narcissus 'Bowles' Early Sulphur'
DAFFODIL

☼ ☼ ❄❄❄❄ ↕20cm (8in) ↔13cm (5in)

Bearing mid-yellow flowers in late winter, this seedling of *N. asturiensis* is one of the earliest-flowering small daffodils. It forms clumps of narrow, strap-shaped leaves.

FLORAL EFFECT

Perennials with a Long Flowering Season

GIVEN THAT MOST GARDEN PERENNIALS, especially during spring, flower for a relatively limited period, it is natural that those with a more extended flowering season should be eagerly sought after by gardeners. These perennials usually bloom throughout summer or from summer into autumn, and will bring an element of continuity to the garden.

FLORAL EFFECT

Astrantia major 'Shaggy'
MASTERWORT
☼ ❆ ❅❆❅ ↕90cm (36in) ↔45cm (18in)

Clusters of tiny flowers, surrounded by large, jagged, green-tipped white bracts, open on branching stems in summer. The deeply cut leaves form bold clumps.

Dicentra 'Stuart Boothman'
DICENTRA
❆ ❅❆❅ ↕30cm (12in) ↔40cm (16in)

A creeping perennial forming clumps of divided, fern-like, blue-grey leaves. Sprays of locket-shaped, pendent, deep pink flowers emerge from spring to summer.

Geranium x *riversleaianum* 'Russell Prichard'
☼ ❆ ❅❆❅ ↕30cm (12in) ↔1m (3ft)

Ideal for ground cover, this low-grower has trailing stems clothed in neatly lobed, sharp-toothed, grey-green leaves. Deep magenta flowers appear in summer.

OTHER PERENNIALS WITH A LONG FLOWERING SEASON

Acanthus spinosus
Anthemis 'Susanna Mitchell'
Aster x *frickartii* 'Mönch', see p.16
Diascia 'Coral Belle'
Geranium wallichianum 'Buxton's Variety'
Lavatera 'Rosea', see p.95
Oenothera speciosa 'Rosea', see p.21
Scabiosa 'Butterfly Blue '
Viola cornuta Alba Group, see p.27

Dianthus deltoides
MAIDEN PINK
☼ ❅❆❅ ↕20cm (8in) ↔30cm (12in)

This reliable pink bears dark-eyed, white, pink, or red flowers throughout summer, above mats of slender, narrow-leaved stems. Thrives on well-drained soil.

Epilobium glabellum of gardens
EPILOBIUM
☼ ❆ ❅❆❅ ↕↔20cm (8in)

During summer, the clumps of arching stems, densely clothed in semi-evergreen leaves, bear creamy white or pink-tinted flowers. Prefers a site in cool, damp shade.

Geum 'Red Wings'
GEUM
☼ ❆ ❅❆❅ ↕60cm (24in) ↔40cm (16in)

Flowering freely throughout summer, this perennial produces semi-double, brilliant scarlet flowers on branched stems, above clumps of softly-hairy, fresh green foliage.

Scabiosa caucasica 'Miss Willmott'
SCABIOUS

☀ ✳✳✳   ↕ 90cm (36in) ↔ 60cm (24in)

Large, solitary white flowerheads, with creamy white centres, adorn the clumps of erect stems in summer. The grey-green stem leaves are deeply divided. ♆

Tradescantia × *andersoniana* 'Isis'
TRADESCANTIA

☀ ☼ ✳✳✳   ↕ ↔ 50cm (20in)

Dense clumps of erect stems, clothed in long-tapering, strap-shaped leaves, carry clusters of large, three-petalled, dark blue flowers from summer to autumn. ♆

Oenothera macrocarpa
OZARK SUNDROPS

☀ ✳✳✳   ↕ 15cm (6in) ↔ 50cm (20in)

Better known as *O. missouriensis*, this vigorous plant has prostrate stems, willowy leaves, and a succession of golden yellow flowers from late spring into autumn. ♆

Phygelius × *rectus* 'African Queen'
CAPE FIGWORT

☀ ✳✳   ↕ 1m (3ft) ↔ 1.4m (4½ft)

A free-flowering plant with loose clumps of four-angled, woody-based stems. The pendent, tubular, pale red flowers, borne in summer, have yellow mouths. ♆

Salvia microphylla
SAGE

☀ ☼ ✳✳✳   ↕ ↔ 1.2m (4ft)

The softly-hairy, evergreen leaves of this woody-based perennial or subshrub smell of blackcurrants when bruised. Its bright red flowers open from summer to autumn.

Viola 'Bowles' Black'
VIOLA

☀ ☼ ✳✳✳✳   ↕ 10cm (4in) ↔ 20cm (8in)

A charming pansy relative with evergreen tufts of leafy stems. It bears a succession of velvety black flowers, with golden eyes, from spring to autumn. Seeds freely.

FLORAL EFFECT

101

Perennials with Flowers in Flattened Heads or Sprays

THERE ARE MANY WAYS of creating interest in a border other than using plants of differing heights or varying foliage. One is to plant perennials that branch horizontally, or have flattened flowerheads or flowers borne along the same plane. These will provide a sharp contrast to plants that have an upright or rounded habit, or bear tall spikes of flowers.

FLORAL EFFECT

Sedum spectabile
ICE PLANT
☼ ❄❄❄   ↕ ↔ 45cm (18in)

This staple of cottage gardens is adored by butterflies and bees. During late summer, flattened heads of pink flowers cover the low mound of fleshy, greyish leaves.   ♈

Achillea 'Coronation Gold'
ACHILLEA
☼ ❄❄❄   ↕ 90cm (36in) ↔ 45cm (18in)

The flattened heads of tiny yellow flowers in summer and autumn are excellent for cutting and drying. Deeply divided, silver-grey leaves form an evergreen clump.   ♈

Chaerophyllum hirsutum 'Roseum'
CHAEROPHYLLUM
☼ ◐ ❄❄❄   ↕ 60cm (24in) ↔ 50cm (20in)

One of the loveliest of its family, it bears flattened, lilac-pink flowerheads in early summer, above clumps of hairy stems covered in ferny, deeply divided leaves.

Selinum wallichianum
SELINUM
☼ ◐ ❄❄❄   ↕ 1.2m (4ft) ↔ 60cm (24in)

A lovely member of the carrot family, with erect stems and divided, ferny leaves. In summer and autumn, tiny white flowers, with black anthers, are borne in flat heads.

Aster lateriflorus 'Horizontalis'
ASTER
☼ ◐ ❄❄❄   ↕ 60cm (24in) ↔ 40cm (16in)

This dense, bushy aster has a distinctive horizontal-branching habit, small leaves, and tiny pink-mauve flowers in autumn, when the leaves turn coppery purple.   ♈

Sambucus ebulus
DANE'S ELDER
☼ ◐ ❄❄❄   ↕ 90cm (36in) ↔ indefinite

Bold, deeply divided leaves clothe this vigorous, suckering elder's erect stems. Its large, sweet-scented white flowerheads in summer are followed by black berries.

OTHER PERENNIALS WITH FLAT HEADS OR SPRAYS OF FLOWERS

Achillea filipendulina 'Gold Plate'
Aster amellus 'King George'
Aster amellus 'Sonia'
Chaerophyllum hirsutum
Heracleum lanatum
Ligularia dentata
Sambucus adnata
Sedum 'Herbstfreude', see p.73
Solidago 'Crown of Rays'
Tanacetum vulgare

Perennials with Flowers in Spikes

PERENNIALS WITH TALL, SPIKE-LIKE HEADS of flowers can create bold and dramatic effects, bringing structure and height to garden displays as they rise above other plants in stiff, tight spires or elegant, tapering racemes. In most flower spikes, the blooms open from the base upwards but some, like those of *Liatris spicata*, open from the top first.

Ligularia 'The Rocket'
LIGULARIA
☼ ☼ ✳✳✳   ↕ 1.8m (6ft) ↔ 1m (3ft)

Tall, black-stemmed spires of tiny yellow flowers rise impressively in summer above the piles of long-stalked, heart-shaped, toothy leaves. Best in moist soil. ♔

Epilobium angustifolium f. *album*
ROSE BAY, WILLOW HERB
☼ ☼ ✳✳✳   ↕ 1.5m (5ft) ↔ 1m (3ft)

The erect stems of this vigorous perennial are clothed in narrow, willow-like leaves, and sport long spires of white flowers with green sepals in summer. Will seed freely.

OTHER PERENNIALS WITH FLOWERS IN SPIKES

Asphodeline lutea, see p.22
Cimicifuga racemosa
Eremurus × *isabellinus* Shelford Hybrids
Heuchera cylindrica
Liatris spicata
Lysimachia ephemerum, see p.131
Lythrum virgatum 'The Rocket'
Verbascum chaixii
Veronicastrum virginicum f. *album*,
   see p.29

Delphinium 'Butterball'
DELPHINIUM
☼ ✳✳✳   ↕ 1.5m (5ft) ↔ 75cm (30in)

In early summer, and sometimes again later, this gorgeous delphinium's sturdy, erect stems bear dense, tapered racemes of semi-double, creamy white flowers.

Digitalis parviflora
RUSTY FOXGLOVE
☼ ✳✳✳   ↕ 1.2m (4ft) ↔ 45cm (18in)

Quite different to the common foxglove (*D. purpurea*), the stiff, architectural spikes of golden brown, red-veined flowers rise above low, leafy rosettes during summer.

Kniphofia 'Erecta'
TORCH LILY
☼ ☼ ✳✳✳   ↕ 90cm (36in) ↔ 60cm (24in)

A robust, clump-forming plant with stiff stems and strap-shaped leaves. The dense pokers of coral-red flowers become erect after opening in late summer and autumn.

Verbascum chaixii 'Album'
NETTLE-LEAVED MULLEIN
☼ ✳✳✳   ↕ 90cm (36in) ↔ 45cm (18in)

Striking and reliable, this mullein bears erect, often branched stems crowded with white, mauve-centred flowers in summer, over semi-evergreen, hairy leaf-rosettes.

Perennials with Hot, Fiery-coloured Flowers

FIERY-COLOURED FLOWERS may not appeal to gardeners with delicate tastes, but for many others, they inject life and passion into the garden. Reflecting the intensity and warmth of the sun, a single fiery-flowered perennial can brighten an otherwise bland border, while combining a few of them in a mixed planting will create a riot of colour.

OTHER PERENNIALS WITH ORANGE FLOWERS

Crocosmia 'Jackanapes'
Euphorbia griffithii 'Fireglow', see p.84
Fritillaria imperialis
Kniphofia 'Prince Igor', see p.23
Kniphofia rooperi
Lilium 'Enchantment'
Lilium superbum
Pilosella aurantiaca
Potentilla 'William Rollison'
Primula bulleyana

Asclepias tuberosa
BUTTERFLY WEED
☼ ✵✵✵ ↕ 90cm (3ft) ↔ 60cm (24in)

It may be a weed in its homeland, but in the garden the glowing orange flowers that crown the erect stems in late summer are a joy. Beware of the caustic, milky sap.

Dahlia 'Bishop of Llandaff'
DAHLIA
☼ ✵ ↕ 1.1m (3½ft) ↔ 45cm (18in)

In late summer, the semi-double, glowing red blooms of this popular perennial are strikingly off-set by its dusky-red stems and leaves. Protect the tubers in winter.

Geum coccineum
GEUM
☼☼ ✵✵✵ ↕ 50cm (20in) ↔ 30cm (12in)

Slender, branching stems carry orange-red flowers, with golden stamens, above a loose clump of deeply divided, hairy green leaves during spring and summer.

Crocosmia masoniorum
MONTBRETIA
☼☼ ✵✵✵ ↕ 1.2m (4ft) ↔ 60cm (24in)

A classic perennial, with bold clumps of sword-shaped, pleated leaves, and arching spikes of trumpet-shaped, rich orange-red flowers in summer. Good for cutting. ♔

Gaillardia 'Dazzler'
BLANKET FLOWER
☼ ✵✵✵ ↕ 75cm (30in) ↔ 45cm (18in)

This bushy, often short-lived perennial has big, daisy flowerheads in summer and early autumn. The orange-red blooms are yellow-tipped with maroon centres. ♔

Helenium 'Septemberfuchs'
HELENIUM
☼ ✵✵✵ ↕ 1.5m (5ft) ↔ 60cm (24in)

In late summer and autumn, stout clumps of erect, leafy stems carry a multitude of bright orange-brown, yellow-suffused daisy-flowers with brown hearts.

Lychnis chalcedonica 'Flore Pleno'
DOUBLE MALTESE CROSS
☼ ❄❄❄ ‡ 1.2m (4ft) ↔ 45cm (18in)

The single-flowered plant is attractive, but this is even better. In summer, erect, hairy, leafy stems bear dense clusters of double scarlet flowers. May need support.

Potentilla 'Monsieur Rouillard'
POTENTILLA
☼ ❄❄❄ ‡ 45cm (18in) ↔ 60cm (24in)

This potentilla has a loose clump of erect or spreading stems with deeply divided leaves. Its double, deep blood-red flowers, with yellow markings, open in summer.

Hemerocallis fulva 'Flore Pleno'
DAYLILY
☼ ☼ ❄❄❄ ‡ 75cm (30in) ↔ 1.2m (4ft)

In summer, erect stems bearing trumpet-shaped, double, orange-brown flowers, with dark red centres, rise above the bold clump of strap-shaped, arching leaves.

Primula 'Inverewe'
CANDELABRA PRIMULA
☼ ☼ ❄❄❄ ‡ ↔ 75cm (30in)

A strong-growing, semi-evergreen primula for damp sites, with a rosette of toothed leaves. Mealy-white stems carry whorls of striking, bright red flowers in summer. ♈

OTHER PERENNIALS WITH RED FLOWERS
Chrysanthemum 'Pennine Signal'
Crocosmia 'Lucifer', see p.116
Geum 'Red Wings', see p.100
Hemerocallis 'Stafford'
Lilium chalcedonicum
Lobelia 'Will Scarlet'
Papaver orientale 'Beauty of Livermere', see p.87
Potentilla 'Flamenco'
Potentilla 'Gibson's Scarlet', see p.75

Kniphofia triangularis
RED HOT POKER
☼ ❄❄❄ ‡ 75cm (30in) ↔ 45cm (18in)

A late-flowering and reliable red hot poker, producing clumps of narrow, grassy leaves, and numerous spikes of reddish orange flowers during autumn. ♈

Monarda 'Squaw'
BERGAMOT
☼ ❄❄❄ ‡ 90cm (36in) ↔ 45cm (18in)

In summer and autumn, the hairy stems, forming bold clumps, bear dense clusters of bright red flowers, loved by bees. The leaves are aromatic when bruised.

Perennials with Cool-coloured Flowers

PINK, BLUE, AND PALE YELLOW are all colours that are cool to the eye, and bring a delicate subtlety to plantings in the garden. White too, plays a similar role, and when used with care and discretion, these cool-coloured flowers can have a soothing, almost therapeutic effect, particularly if they bloom during the heat of summer.

FLORAL EFFECT

Centaurea pulcherrima
CENTAUREA
☀ ❄❄❄   ↕ 40cm (16in) ↔ 60cm (24in)

Slender stems rise from clumps of deeply lobed or entire, woolly-backed leaves to bear lovely rose-pink, pale-centred corn-flowers from late spring to early summer.

OTHER PERENNIALS WITH EARLY, COOL-COLOURED FLOWERS

Aquilegia 'Hensol Harebell'
Corydalis flexuosa 'China Blue', see p.65
Dicentra spectabilis 'Alba', see p.108
Epimedium × *versicolor* 'Sulphureum'
Omphalodes cappadocica 'Cherry Ingram'
   Paeonia mlokosewitschii, see p.149
   Polemonium caeruleum
Pulmonaria 'Mawson's Blue', see p.91
Veratrum album, see p.85

Agapanthus 'Snowy Owl'
AFRICAN LILY
☀ ☼ ❄❄❄   ↕ 1.2m (4ft) ↔ 60cm (24in)

In late summer, sturdy stems carry large, loosely rounded umbels of bell-shaped, pure white flowers above the bold clumps of narrow, strap-shaped green leaves.

Astilbe 'Venus'
ASTILBE
☀ ☼ ☼ ❄❄❄   ↕ 90cm (36in) ↔ 45cm (18in)

Large, frothy, conical plumes of tiny pink flowers rise above robust clumps of much-divided, bright green, handsome leaves in early summer. It prefers a moist soil.

Anchusa azurea 'Loddon Royalist'
ALKANET
☀ ❄❄❄   ↕ 90cm (36in) ↔ 60cm (24in)

The branched heads of attractive, deep blue flowers, with white bird's-eyes, top tall, sturdy clumps of erect, rough-hairy and leafy stems during early summer. ♛

Campanula persicifolia 'Telham Beauty'
☀ ☼ ❄❄❄   ↕ 90cm (36in) ↔ 30cm (12in)

A lovely form of a popular, cottage-garden perennial, the tall, slender stems bearing racemes of large, light blue bell-flowers in summer. Both easy to grow and reliable.

Chrysanthemum 'Clara Curtis'
CHRYSANTHEMUM
☀ ❄❄❄   ↕ 75cm (30in) ↔ 60cm (24in)

Fine-cut leaves cover the bushy, woody-based clump of stems. The scented, long-lasting, clear pink daisy-heads are borne freely from late summer into autumn.

Delphinium 'Blue Bees'
DELPHINIUM
☼ ❄❄❄   ↕ 1m (3ft) ↔ 45cm (18in)

The upright, branching, wiry stems bear
deeply cut leaves, and racemes of long-
spurred, clear blue, white-eyed flowers in
early summer and again in late summer.

Gentiana asclepiadea
WILLOW GENTIAN
☼ ☼ ❄❄❄ ↕ 90cm (36in) ↔ 60cm (12in)

Pairs of willow-like leaves clothe the bold
clumps of arching stems. Pale or deep
blue flowers emerge from the upper leaf
axils from late summer to autumn. ♆

Iris winogradowii
IRIS
☼ ❄❄❄   ↕ 7.5cm (3in) ↔ 10cm (4in)

In early spring, primrose-yellow flowers,
with green-flecked falls, rise above tufts
of four-sided, slender leaves. Excellent for
containers, troughs, or a rock garden.

Monarda 'Croftway Pink'
BERGAMOT
☼ ☼ ❄❄❄ ↕ 90cm (36in) ↔ 60cm (24in)

Popular with bees, this aromatic perennial
has erect stems clothed in paired leaves.
In summer, it freely bears clusters of clear
rose-pink flowers with dark bracts. ♆

Paeonia 'Sarah Bernhardt'
PEONY
☼ ☼ ❄❄❄   ↕ ↔ 90cm (36in)

This robust perennial produces clumps of
erect, leafy stems, which bear very large,
fragrant, fully double, rose-pink blooms in
early summer. Excellent for cutting. ♆

Penstemon heterophyllus
'Blue Gem'
☼ ☼ ❄❄❄   ↕ ↔ 40cm (16in)

Striking in flower, this evergreen or semi-
evergreen, woody-based perennial bears
slender, glossy leaves, and dense, erect
racemes of tubular blue summer flowers.

**OTHER PERENNIALS WITH LATE,
COOL-COLOURED FLOWERS**

Agapanthus 'Dorothy Palmer'
Geranium x *oxonianum* 'A.T. Johnson'
Liatris spicata 'Floristan Weiss'
Oenothera stricta 'Sulphurea', see p.29
Phlox paniculata 'Fujiyama', see p.109
Phygelius x *rectus* 'Moonraker'
Platycodon grandiflorus f. *albus*
Salvia uliginosa
Schizostylis coccinea 'Viscountess Byng',
   see p.69

Sidalcea 'Elsie Heugh'
CHECKERBLOOM
☼ ❄❄❄ ↕ 90cm (36in) ↔ 45cm (18in)

A reliable plant with erect or spreading
stems bearing deeply lobed stem leaves,
and tall racemes of long-lasting, satiny,
purple-pink mallow-flowers in summer.

Perennials with Pale-coloured Flowers

PALE-COLOURED FLOWERS can provide one of the most effective means of illuminating a dark corner or shaded border in the garden. Shining out against a backdrop of dark foliage, they attract and reflect any available light, and can even draw attention to borders and beds at the end of the day when darkness is falling.

Dictamnus albus
BURNING BUSH
☼ ☼ ✳✳✳✳ ↕ 90cm (36in) ↔ 60cm (24in)

A slow-growing plant forming clumps of deeply divided, aromatic foliage, and in early summer bold, erect racemes of white flowers with conspicuous stamens. ♈

Coreopsis verticillata 'Moonbeam'
TICKSEED
☼ ☼ ✳✳✳✳ ↕ 50cm (20in) ↔ 45cm (18in)

In summer, a profusion of lemon-yellow flowerheads covers this low, bushy plant. Its slender, branched stems bear finely cut leaves. Ideal for the front of a border.

OTHER PERENNIALS WITH PALE-COLOURED FLOWERS

Cephalaria gigantea, see p.72
Iris 'Cliffs of Dover'
Kniphofia 'Maid of Orleans'
Leucanthemum × *superbum* 'Wirral Pride', see p.79
Oenothera speciosa 'Rosea', see p.21
Persicaria bistorta 'Superba'
Polemonium carneum
Potentilla recta var. *pallida*
Ranunculus bulbosus 'F.M. Burton'

Anthemis tinctoria 'Sauce Hollandaise'
ANTHEMIS
☼ ✳✳✳ ↕ ↔ 60cm (24in)

Long-stalked, yellow-centred, pale cream daisy-heads are borne freely over many weeks during summer, above clumps of finely divided, dark green leaves.

Campanula persicifolia 'Chettle Charm'
PEACH-LEAVED BELLFLOWER
☼ ☼ ✳✳✳✳ ↕ 90cm (36in) ↔ 30cm (12in)

One of the loveliest varieties of a popular perennial, with tall, slender stems, narrow leaves, and loose sprays of pale summer bell-flowers, tinged blue at the edges.

Dicentra spectabilis 'Alba'
BLEEDING HEART
☼ ✳✳✳✳ ↕ 60cm (24in) ↔ 45cm (18in)

This beautiful and elegant perennial has ferny, pale green foliage, and produces long stems hung with locket-shaped white flowers from late spring to summer. ♈

Gaura lindheimeri
GAURA
☼ ☼ ✳✳✳✳ ↕ 1.2m (4ft) ↔ 90cm (36in)

Branched, willowy stems of slender leaves give this gaura a bushy, loose habit. Pink buds open to elegant sprays of white star-flowers in late summer and autumn. ♈

Phlox paniculata 'Fujiyama'
BORDER PHLOX
☼ ☼ ❄❄❄ ↕ 90cm (36in) ↔ 60cm (24in)

Impressive, large heads of snow-white
flowers crown the stout clumps of upright,
leafy stems in late summer. This is one of
the best perennials for white flowers. ♈

Gillenia trifoliata
INDIAN PHYSIC
☼ ☼ ❄❄❄ ↕ 1m (3ft) ↔ 60cm (24in)

Wiry, reddish stems bear divided, bronze-
green leaves, and sprays of small white
flowers in spring and summer. Decorative
red calyces remain after the petals fall. ♈

Phygelius aequalis 'Yellow Trumpet'
PHYGELIUS
☼ ❄❄ ↕ 1m (3ft) ↔ 1.2m (4ft)

This strong-grower has clumps of four-
angled, woody-based, leafy stems bearing
loose racemes of drooping, tubular, pale
yellow flowers in summer and autumn. ♈

Kirengeshoma palmata
KIRENGESHOMA
☼ ❄❄❄ ↕ 1.2m (4ft) ↔ 75cm (30in)

A handsome perennial with dark stems
and large, boldly toothed or lobed leaves.
Sprays of waxy, pale yellow flowers are
borne in autumn. It enjoys moist soil. ♈

Kniphofia 'Little Maid'
TORCH LILY
☼ ☼ ❄❄❄ 60cm (24in) ↔ 45cm (18in)

In autumn, erect stems rise from clumps
of grassy leaves to bear long, dense spikes
of tubular, buff-tinted yellow flowers, pale
green in bud, and fading to ivory. ♈

Trollius x *cultorum* 'Alabaster'
GLOBEFLOWER
☼ ☼ ❄❄❄ ↕ 60cm (24in) ↔ 40cm (16in)

Beautiful, rounded, pale primrose-yellow
flowers rise on long stems above clumps
of long-stalked, lobed, glossy leaves from
late spring to summer. It likes moist soil.

Perennials with Fragrant Flowers

IT IS OFTEN SURPRISING to find that a beautiful flower does not have a scent to match. However, most highly fragrant perennials have relatively small flowers, and those with large, scented blooms are frequently white or pale coloured. Many fragrant flowers are at their best at the end of the day, when night-flying pollinators visit the garden.

Dianthus 'Doris'
MODERN PINK
☼ ❄❄❄ ↕↔40cm (16in)

Double, pale pink, dark-centred flowers top the blue-grey, bloomy, narrow-leaved stems of this much-loved and reliable pink in summer and early autumn. 🏆

Hemerocallis 'Marion Vaughn'
DAYLILY
☼ ◐ ❄❄❄ ↕85cm (34in) ↔75cm (30in)

During summer, clusters of very fragrant, lemon-yellow trumpet-flowers are borne freely on erect stems above bold clumps of semi-evergreen, strap-shaped leaves. 🏆

Iris graminea
PLUM TART IRIS
☼ ◐ ❄❄❄ ↕40cm (16in) ↔30cm (12in)

During late spring and early summer, the small, violet-purple flowers of this clump-forming, grassy-leaved iris give off a distinct, fruity fragrance, like hot plums.

PERENNIALS WITH FRAGRANT WINTER AND SPRING FLOWERS

Convallaria majalis
Crocus laevigatus
Erysimum cheiri 'Harpur Crewe'
Galanthus 'Brenda Troyle'
Galanthus 'S. Arnott'
Hyacinthoides non-scripta
Iris unguicularis
Narcissus jonquilla
Narcissus x *odorus* 'Rugulosus'
Petasites fragrans
Viola odorata

Erysimum cheiri 'Blood Red'
WALLFLOWER
☼ ❄❄❄ ↕80cm (32in) ↔40cm (16in)

The scent of wallflowers is one of the joys of spring. Although short-lived, they are available in many flower colours. This one bears striking, rich blood-red blooms.

Hosta 'Honeybells'
PLANTAIN LILY
◐ ● ❄❄❄ ↕75cm (30in) ↔1.2m (4ft)

A vigorous clump-former with attractive, heart-shaped, veined, and wavy-margined leaves. Fragrant white or lavender-blue-streaked flowers open in late summer. 🏆

Lilium regale
REGAL LILY
☼ ❄❄❄ ↕1.5m (5ft) ↔40cm (16in)

One of the most famous of fragrant lilies, this is a must for sunny gardens. Robust stems flaunt bold clusters of white, pink-striped trumpet-flowers in summer. 🏆

Narcissus poeticus var. *recurvus*
OLD PHEASANT'S EYE
☼ ☼ ❄❄❄ ↕ 35cm (14in) ↔ 30cm (12in)

Beautiful, crisp white flowers with pale yellow, red-rimmed cups rise above the narrow, strap-shaped leaves in late spring. In time, it forms clumps or patches. ♈

Nicotiana sylvestris
ORNAMENTAL TOBACCO PLANT
☼ ☼ ❄ ↕ 1.5m (5ft) ↔ 60cm (24in)

The bold, leafy stems carry large heads of long-tubed, fragrant white flowers during summer. Perennial in warm sites, it is best treated as biennial in colder areas. ♈

> **PERENNIALS WITH FRAGRANT SUMMER FLOWERS**
>
> *Cosmos atrosanguineus*
> *Dianthus* 'Lavender Clove'
> *Hemerocallis lilioasphodelus*
> *Hesperis matronalis*
> *Hosta plantaginea* var. *grandiflora*
> *Hosta* 'Summer Fragrance'
> *Lilium candidum*
> *Paeonia* 'Festiva Maxima'
> *Phlox maculata* 'Omega'
> *Primula florindae*

Phlox maculata 'Alpha'
MEADOW PHLOX
☼ ☼ ❄❄❄ ↕ 90cm (36in) ↔ 60cm (24in)

More elegant than the popular border variety, this phlox produces erect clumps of leafy stems, which bear large heads of fragrant pink flowers during summer. ♈

Primula auricula var. *albocincta*
AURICULA
☼ ☼ ❄❄❄ ↕ ↔ 20cm (8in)

Gorgeous for a rock garden or container, with clumps of evergreen, greyish, white-edged leaves topped by umbels of yellow, white-eyed, scented flowers in spring.

Tulbaghia violacea
TULBAGHIA
☼ ❄❄❄ ↕ 50cm (20in) ↔ 25cm (10in)

Erect stems carry loose umbels of fragrant lilac flowers in summer and early autumn over clumps of narrow, grey-green leaves. It will thrive in a warm, sunny site.

Verbena corymbosa 'Gravetye'
VERBENA
☼ ❄❄ ↕ 90cm (3ft) ↔ 60cm (24in)

Beautiful when in flower, this perennial produces dense heads of pinkish purple, white-eyed flowers throughout summer, which give off a sweet perfume.

FOLIAGE EFFECT

WHILE MOST FLOWERS bloom for a relatively brief period, foliage can provide a continuous source of drama and atmosphere in the garden. Perennials that have contrasting leaf shapes, textures, and colours will enliven beds and borders, and can also make a striking display as specimen plants.

Hosta 'Big Daddy' for bold foliage

△ DELICATE CONTRAST *A feathery-leaved* Dicentra *complements the silver-splashed, rounded foliage of a* Lamium.

Foliage provides a constant focus in the garden, acting as both a foil for flowers and a firm basis for design. Perennials in this section offer a huge range of leaf shapes, colours, and arrangements which, used thoughtfully or with flair, can be combined for spectacular effects. Large-leaved perennials, such as ornamental rhubarbs (*Rheum*), can make impressive specimen plants, or add structure and impact to beds and borders. Foliage perennials will also prove their worth in containers, providing a satisfying, long-lasting display that can be moved around the garden. Richly tinted foliage is often associated with autumn, but it is worth remembering that many perennials offer leaves that are attractively variegated or coloured for much of the year. Excellent for brightening a dull border, they are also useful for shady sites where other plants may struggle to flower without sufficient sun. In winter, when most other perennials lie below ground, those with evergreen or overwintering leaves, such as bergenias and hardy ferns, can also be used to bring interest and life to the garden landscape.

FOLIAGE CHARACTERISTICS

Leaf arrangement, shape, and colour are all important elements to consider when combining foliage perennials for eye-catching contrasts and effects.

ARRANGEMENT *of leaves is a characteristic feature of every plant. Exploit this to bring structure and texture to the garden.*

SHAPE AND SIZE *can be contrasted for extra interest. Leaves with jagged, feathery, or spiny margins will all create different effects.*

COLOUR *in foliage can be used to create a calm, dark backdrop, or to bring brightness and warmth to shady sites in the garden.*

◁ COLOUR CONTAINER *Yellow-striped* Hakonechloa *and blue-leaved* Acaena *contrast here with upright* Imperata.

▷ DRAMATIC LEAVES *Perennials with bold foliage make good specimen plants or can be used to great effect in a border.*

Perennials with Evergreen or Overwintering Foliage

I N WINTER, when most herbaceous perennials have died down to below ground level and no longer provide a focus in the garden, it is important to have at least a scattering of plants with evergreen leaves or foliage that overwinters in an attractive state. Even when flowerless, these plants will bring continual colour and interest to any garden.

Asarum europāeum
ASARABACCA
☼ ☀ ❋❋❋ ↕ 8cm (3in) ↔ 30cm (12in)

One of the best perennials for ground cover, and attractive all year round. In late spring, the dense carpet of kidney-shaped, glossy leaves hides curious little flowers.

Helleborus argutifolius
CORSICAN HELLEBORE
☼ ☀ ❋❋❋ ↕ ↔ 90cm (36in)

This handsome plant can be admired all year. Pale green, overwintering stems bear beautifully veined, prickle-toothed leaves, and apple-green flowers in late winter. ♔

Kniphofia caulescens
RED HOT POKER
☼ ☀ ❋❋❋ ↕ 1.2m (4ft) ↔ 90cm (36in)

An impressive kniphofia, producing large clumps of fine-toothed, blue-green leaves, topped in late summer by imposing, coral-red flower spikes, fading to yellow. ♔

Bergenia cordifolia 'Purpurea'
ELEPHANT'S EAR
☼ ☀ ❋❋❋ ↕ 60cm (24in) ↔ 75cm (30in)

The leathery, rounded, deep green leaves form a low patch, becoming purple- or red-tinted in winter. In winter and early spring, it has magenta-purple flowers. ♔

Iris foetidissima 'Variegata'
GLADWYN
☼ ☀ ❋❋❋ ↕ ↔ 60cm (24in)

A superb, variegated form of the gladwyn, its evergreen, strap-shaped, shiny leaves are boldly margined white. Orange seed-heads follow the purple summer flowers.

Phormium cookianum subsp. *hookeri* 'Tricolor'
☼ ❋❋ ↕ ↔ 2m (6ft)

One of the most colourful evergreen perennials, developing a large mound of arching, leathery, glossy green leaves with creamy yellow and red margins. ♔

Polypodium vulgare 'Cornubiense'
POLYPODY
☼ ☼ ❋❋❋❋   ↕ ↔ 40cm (16in)

The much-divided, rich green fronds of
this strong-growing, creeping fern provide
excellent ground cover. It is also suitable
for a rock garden, wall, or container.

Tellima grandiflora
FRINGE CUPS
☼ ❋❋❋❋   ↕ 80cm (32in) ↔ 30cm (12in)

The clump of long-stalked, heart-shaped,
hairy and scalloped leaves will overwinter
in all but severe conditions. Loose spikes
of greenish white flowers appear in spring.

**OTHER EVERGREEN OR OVER-
WINTERING PERENNIALS**

Astelia chathamica
Bergenia 'Bressingham Ruby'
Epimedium pinnatum subsp. *colchicum*,
  see p.46
Galax urceolata
Helleborus foetidus 'Wester Flisk',
  see p.99
Iris japonica
Liriope muscari 'Variegata'
Phlomis russeliana
Phormium tenax, see p.117
Polystichum munitum, see p.140
Polystichum setiferum Divisilobum
  Group
Reineckia carnea
Santolina chamaecyparissus
Shibataea kumasasa
Yucca filamentosa

Pulmonaria saccharata 'Leopard'
PULMONARIA
☼ ◐ ❋❋❋❋   ↕ 30cm (12in) ↔ 60cm (24in)

One of the best overwintering, silvery-
spotted pulmonarias, it makes particularly
effective ground cover. Violet-red flowers
are produced from winter to late spring.

Vinca minor 'Argenteovariegata'
PERIWINKLE
☼ ☼ ❋❋❋❋   ↕ 15cm (6in) ↔ indefinite

All periwinkles are useful as ground cover,
but this also has leaves with attractive,
creamy white margins. Pale violet-blue
flowers open in spring and autumn. ♈

FOLIAGE EFFECT

Perennials with Strap- or Sword-shaped Leaves

PERENNIALS WITH CLUMPS of long, narrow leaves are irresistible and always striking. Regardless of whether the leaves stand stiff and upright, or bend and arch in a more graceful manner, they are valuable for contrasting with more conventional, broad-leaved perennials in beds or borders, and can also be used as dramatic specimen plants.

Iris pseudacorus 'Variegata'
YELLOW FLAG
☼ ☼ ❄❄❄ ↕ ↔ 1.2m (4ft)

A vigorous iris for wet sites, forming a large patch of tall green leaves with bold white or creamy yellow bands. In summer, yellow flowers are borne on erect stems.

EVERGREEN PERENNIALS WITH STRAP- OR SWORD-SHAPED LEAVES

Beschorneria yuccoides
Crocosmia paniculata
Dianella tasmanica
Eryngium eburneum, see p.22
Eryngium pandanifolium
Iris confusa
Iris foetidissima
Watsonia pillansii
Yucca filamentosa
Yucca recurvifolia

Arundo donax 'Macrophylla'
ARUNDO
☼ ❄❄❄ ↕ 5m (15ft) ↔ 2m (6ft)

This giant, evergreen grass produces long, arching, glaucous leaves, and bamboo-like stems flaunting feathery plumes in summer. It prefers a warm, sheltered site.

Eryngium agavifolium
ERYNGIUM
☼ ❄❄ ↕ 1.2m (4ft) ↔ 60cm (24in)

The sharply toothed, glossy, evergreen leaves form a striking, erect clump, above which sturdy stems carry cylindrical heads of tiny, greenish white flowers in summer.

Crocosmia 'Lucifer'
MONTBRETIA
☼ ☼ ❄❄ ↕ 1.2m (4ft) ↔ 45cm (18in)

A bright and cheerful perennial, forming a clump of robust, sword-shaped leaves. Its arching, branched spikes of brilliant red, late-summer flowers are good for cutting.

Hemerocallis 'Gentle Shepherd'
DAYLILY
☼ ☼ ❄❄❄ ↕ 65cm (26in) ↔ 1.2m (4ft)

During summer, the bold clump of semi-evergreen, narrow, arching green leaves is topped by wide-spreading, ivory-white flowers with green throats.

Iris sibirica 'Perry's Blue'
IRIS
☼ ☼ ❄❄❄ ↕ 1.2m (4ft) ↔ 1m (3ft)

Erect clumps of narrow, grass-like leaves are joined in early summer by blue-violet flowers on upright, soldier-like stems. Its winter seed capsules are also decorative.

Sisyrinchium striatum 'Aunt May'
SISYRINCHIUM
☼ ❋❋❋   ↕ 50cm (20in) ↔ 30cm (12in)

This iris-like perennial has striking fans of sword-shaped, grey-green leaves, boldly striped creamy yellow. In summer, it bears straw-yellow flowers in stiff spikes.

Kniphofia 'Wrexham Buttercup'
TORCH LILY
☼ ❋❋❋   ↕ 1.2m (4ft) ↔ 60cm (24in)

The long, arching, narrow green leaves of this perennial form a dense clump. Its poker-like heads of rich yellow flowers are carried on strong stems in summer.

Yucca flaccida
YUCCA
☼ ❋❋❋   ↕ 55cm (22in) ↔ 1.5m (5ft)

Reliable and evergreen, this yucca forms a bold rosette of narrow, dark blue-green leaves with wispy marginal fibres. Large heads of ivory flowers emerge in summer.

HERBACEOUS PERENNIALS WITH STRAP- OR SWORD-SHAPED LEAVES

Agapanthus 'Blue Giant', see p.84
Asphodelus albus
Bletilla striata
Crinum x *powellii*, see p.40
Crocosmia 'Emily McKenzie'
Gladiolus communis subsp. *byzantinus*, see p.33
Hemerocallis fulva 'Europa'
Iris 'Shelford Giant'
Kniphofia 'Royal Standard'
Moraea spathulata
Nerine bowdenii

Persicaria macrophylla
PERSICARIA
☼ ☼ ❋❋❋   ↕ ↔ 30cm (12in)

A semi-evergreen perennial with lance-shaped, conspicuously veined leaves, and dense spikes of pink to red flowers borne through summer into autumn.

Phormium tenax
NEW ZEALAND FLAX
☼ ❋❋❋   ↕ 4m (12ft) ↔ 2m (6ft)

Few perennials are as eye-catching as this flax, with its sword-shaped, glaucous-grey, evergreen leaves, and statuesque panicles of waxy, dark red flowers in summer. ♔

FOLIAGE EFFECT

117

Perennials with Deep-cut or Jagged Leaves

THE NUMBER OF PERENNIALS with bold, entire leaves has led to an increase in demand for plants that have deeply cut, divided, or jaggedly cut foliage to use with them as a contrast. Fortunately, their number and variety are great, and many of them also have the added advantage of attractive flowers.

Rodgersia henrici
RODGERSIA
☼ ☼ ✳✳✳   ↕ ↔ 1m (3ft)

All rodgersias sport handsome foliage, but this one is particularly desirable. It has large, horse-chestnut-like leaves, and pink or white flower plumes in summer.

 *Astilbe* 'Bronze Elegans'
ASTILBE
☼ ☼ ✳✳✳   ↕ 30cm (12in) ↔ 25cm (10in)

One of the smallest and daintiest astilbes, forming hummocks of ferny, glossy, dark green leaves, and neat little plumes of pinkish red flowers in late summer. ♔

Incarvillea delavayi
INCARVILLEA
☼ ☼ ✳✳✳   ↕ 60cm (24in) ↔ 30cm (12in)

Already attractive with its clump of bold, deeply divided, dark green leaves, this plant really catches the eye in summer when its rose-pink trumpet-flowers open.

Senecio tanguticus
CHINESE RAGWORT
☼ ☼ ✳✳✳   ↕ 1.2m (4ft) ↔ indefinite

The creeping rootstock produces stout, dark stems clothed in jaggedly cut leaves. In autumn, substantial, conical heads of yellow flowers emerge. It can be invasive.

OTHER PERENNIALS WITH DEEP-CUT OR JAGGED LEAVES

Acanthus spinosus
Aconitum japonicum
Astrantia major 'Shaggy', see p.100
Kirengeshoma palmata, see p.109
Ligularia japonica
Podophyllum peltatum
Rheum palmatum var. *tanguticum*, see p.123
Rodgersia pinnata, see p.61
Rodgersia podophylla, see p.133

Cimicifuga simplex Atropurpurea Group
BUGBANE
☼ ✳✳✳   ↕ 1.2m (4ft) ↔ 60cm (24in)

The loose clumps of large, much-divided, dark green to purplish leaves are topped during autumn by long, cylindrical, dark-stemmed racemes of tiny white flowers.

Ligularia przewalskii
LIGULARIA
☼ ☼ ✳✳✳   ↕ 2m (6ft) ↔ 1m (3ft)

Easily recognized, this robust perennial develops large clumps of rounded, sharply divided, deep-cut leaves. Dark-stemmed spires of yellow flowers open in summer.

Perennials with Feathery Foliage

SOME PERENNIALS HAVE LEAVES so finely divided that they create a striking feathery or ferny effect. This provides the perfect foil for more dramatic foliage, or for hot-coloured flowers that stand out against the delicate leaves. Many will also make excellent specimen plants in a prominent site in the garden, or featured in containers.

Meum athamanticum
BALDMONEY, SPIGNEL
☼ ❉❉❉ ↕ 45cm (18in) ↔ 30cm (12in)

Like fennel, this is a member of the carrot family, with similarly feathery, deeply divided, aromatic leaves. Dense heads of tiny white flowers are borne in summer.

Adiantum pedatum
MAIDENHAIR FERN
☼ ❉❉❉ ↕ ↔ 40cm (16in)

Given time and a sheltered, moist site, this lovely, hardy fern will develop a large clump of slender, glossy black stalks with delicate, much-divided fronds. ♔

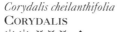

Corydalis cheilanthifolia
CORYDALIS
☼ ☼ ❉❉❉❉ ↕ 30cm (12in) ↔ 25cm (10in)

Each finely divided, orange-tinted leaf is like a green feather. Slender racemes of deep yellow flowers are borne in spring and summer. It will seed around if happy.

> **OTHER PERENNIALS WITH FEATHERY FOLIAGE**
>
> *Achillea millefolium* 'Cerise Queen'
> *Adiantum venustum*
>   Adonis vernalis, see p.98
>   *Argyranthemum gracile* 'Chelsea Girl'
>   *Artemisia alba* 'Canescens'
>   Equisetum sylvaticum
>   Paesia scaberula
> *Polystichum setiferum*
>   Plumosodivisilobum Group
> *Pulsatilla vulgaris*

Aruncus aethusifolius
ARUNCUS
☼ ☼ ❉❉❉ ↕ 25cm (10in) ↔ 40cm (16in)

A charming plant with small hummocks of finely divided, crisp green leaves, which turn orange or yellow in autumn. Small white flower plumes are borne in summer.

Foeniculum vulgare 'Purpureum'
PURPLE FENNEL
☼ ❉❉❉ ↕ 1.8m (6ft) ↔ 45cm (18in)

This aromatic fennel has finely divided, plumed leaves, which are bronze-purple when young, ageing to blue-green. Flat heads of yellow flowers open in summer.

Onychium japonicum
CARROT FERN
☼ ☼ ❉❉❉ ↕ 50cm (20in) ↔ 30cm (12in)

An elegant fern, producing a dense clump of finely divided, bright green fronds on slender, wiry stalks. Some variants are less hardy and are best cultivated under glass.

FOLIAGE EFFECT

119

Perennials with Spiny Leaves

THE JAGGED EFFECT of spiny or prickly leaved plants has a definite appeal for some gardeners. Often architectural in habit, as well as ornamental, these distinctive plants can bring structure to borders or make bold specimens. Many are particularly useful for dry sites, as their spiny leaves are specially adapted to minimize water loss.

Eryngium variifolium
ERYNGO
☼ ❄❄❄ ↕ 35cm (14in) ↔ 25cm (10in)

A beautiful evergreen, forming a rosette of rounded, silver-veined leaves. In summer, erect, branched stems bear small, grey-blue flowerheads with spiny white collars.

OTHER PERENNIALS WITH SPINY LEAVES
Aciphylla colensoi
Berkheya macrocephala
Circium japonicum
Circium rivulare 'Atropurpureum'
Echinops sphaerocephalus
Eryngium proteiflorum
Festuca punctoria
Juncus acutus
Puya alpestris, see p.41
Yucca gloriosa, see p.31

Acanthus spinosus Spinosissimus Group
☼ ◐ ❄❄❄ ↕ 1.2m (4ft) ↔ 60cm (24in)

The large, deeply divided, green or grey-green leaves have white midribs and spiny margins. Tall racemes of purple-bracted white flowers open in spring and summer.

Aciphylla aurea
GOLDEN SPANIARD
☼ ❄❄❄ ↕↔ 1m (3ft)

This slow-growing, evergreen plant forms an imposing rosette of stiff, spine-tipped, deeply divided, grey-green leaves with bold, golden yellow midribs and margins.

Eryngium maritimum
SEA HOLLY
☼ ❄❄❄ ↕↔ 30cm (12in)

Found in maritime sands or gravels in the wild, this sea holly has formidably spiny, deeply lobed, leathery, bloomy, blue-grey leaves. Pale blue flowers open in summer.

Puya chilensis
PUYA
☼ ❄❄❄ ↕ 4m (12ft) ↔ 2m (6ft)

After several years, a tall, stout stem with a head of waxy, yellow-green flowers rises from the massive rosette of rapier-like, spine-toothed, leathery, evergreen leaves.

Perennials with Aromatic Leaves

SCENTS CAN MAKE an important and evocative contribution to a garden, and are most commonly associated with the fragrance of flowers. The leaves of most perennials, however, also give off at least a faint aroma, and some even have foliage with a very distinctive or strong scent. In a number of cases, this is released by simply brushing against the plant.

Nepeta 'Six Hills Giant'
CATMINT
☼ ◐ ❄❄❄ ↕ 90cm (36in) ↔ 60cm (24in)

This dense, bushy, clump-forming plant bears aromatic, light grey-green leaves, and leafy spikes of lavender-blue summer flowers. Loved, but also damaged, by cats.

Agastache foeniculum 'Alabaster'
ANISE HYSSOP
☼ ❄❄❄ ↕ 90cm (36in) ↔ 30cm (12in)

Downy, anise-scented leaves, paler green beneath, clothe the erect stems. Spikes of two-lipped white flowers, loved by bees, are borne from midsummer to autumn.

Helichrysum italicum
HELICHRYSUM
☼ ❄❄❄ ↕ 60cm (24in) ↔ 90cm (36in)

Aromatic, evergreen, narrow, felted, silver-grey leaves clothe the woolly stems of this woody-based perennial or subshrub. Deep yellow flowerheads open in summer. ♈

OTHER PERENNIALS WITH AROMATIC LEAVES
Acorus calamus 'Variegatus'
Foeniculum vulgare 'Purpureum', see p.119
Helichrysum italicum subsp. *serotinum*
Ipheion uniflorum 'Wisley Blue'
Melittis melissophyllum, see p.73
Mentha x *gracilis* 'Variegata'
Mentha x *piperita* f. *citrata*
Mentha suaveolens 'Variegata'
Myrrhis odorata, see p.49
Origanum vulgare
Perovskia 'Blue Spire', see p.23

Chamaemelum nobile 'Flore Pleno'
CHAMOMILE
☼ ❄❄❄ ↕ 30cm (12in) ↔ 45cm (18in)

This small, creeping, aromatic perennial produces dense mats of finely divided, hairy leaves. Long-stalked, double white flowerheads are borne freely in summer.

Melissa officinalis
LEMON BALM
☼ ◐ ❄❄❄ ↕ 1m (3ft) ↔ 60cm (24in)

When rubbed, the leaves of this bushy perennial release a sharp lemon aroma. In summer, its four-angled stems bear spikes of pale yellow flowers that fade to white.

Salvia officinalis 'Icterina'
SAGE
☼ ❄❄❄ ↕ ↔ 30cm (12in)

A variegated form of the popular kitchen-garden herb, forming a low, woody-based mound of attractive, aromatic, evergreen, woolly, green and yellow leaves. ♈

121

Perennials with Bold Leaves

PERENNIALS WITH BIG, BOLD LEAVES, like those of hostas and ornamental rhubarbs, provide gardens with some of the most memorable show-stoppers. In sites where space is no object, they are eye-catching planted in groups or drifts, but they can be just as successful, and possibly even more dramatic, as single specimens in smaller gardens.

OTHER HERBACEOUS PERENNIALS
WITH BOLD LEAVES

Darmera peltata, see p.60
Filipendula kamtschatica
Gunnera manicata
Hedychium gardnerianum, see p.41
Hosta sieboldiana
Inula magnifica
Petasites japonicus var. *giganteus*
Rodgersia aesculifolia, see p.19
Silphium terebinthinaceum
Veratrum album, see p.85

Aralia cachemirica
ARALIA
☼ ◑ ❋❋❋   ↕ 3m (10ft) ↔ 2m (6ft)

Given a good site, this aralia forms a huge, suckering clump of large, arching, divided leaves. Black berries follow tall, branched heads of tiny flowers in early summer.

Dicksonia antarctica
AUSTRALIAN TREE FERN
☼ ◑ ❋❋   ↕ 6m (20ft) ↔ 4m (12ft)

This majestic, evergreen fern has a single rhizome forming a false, erect trunk, which is clothed in a thick mass of roots and crowned with a huge ruff of fronds. ♆

Astilboides tabularis
ASTILBOIDES
◑ ❋❋❋   ↕ 1.5m (5ft) ↔ 1.2m (4ft)

In summer, slender plumes of tiny, creamy white flowers rise above the big clumps of long-stalked, rounded, sharply lobed, and softly-downy leaves. It enjoys moist soils.

OTHER EVERGREEN PERENNIALS
WITH BOLD LEAVES

Beschorneria yuccoides
Geranium maderense
Helleborus argutifolius, see p.114
Indocalamus tessellatus
Phormium cookianum subsp. *hookeri*
  'Tricolor', see p.114
Phormium tenax, see p.117
Wachendorfia thyrsiflora
Woodwardia unigemmata
Yucca gloriosa, see p.31

Filipendula purpurea
FILIPENDULA
☼ ◑ ❋❋❋   ↕ 1.2m (4ft) ↔ 60cm (24in)

Large, deeply lobed and toothed leaves cover the bold clumps of erect, crimson-purple stems. In summer, tall, branched plumes of carmine-red flowers appear. ♆

FOLIAGE EFFECT

122

Geranium palmatum
CRANESBILL
☀ ☀ ❄❄❄   ↕ ↔ 1m (3ft)

Branched heads of purplish pink flowers
top the large rosettes of long-stalked,
sharp-toothed, deeply lobed, evergreen
leaves in summer. ♛

Hosta 'Big Daddy'
PLANTAIN LILY
☀ ☀ ❄❄❄   ↕ 60cm (24in) ↔ 1m (3ft)

Aptly named, this hosta has mounded
clumps of large, rounded to heart-shaped,
veined and puckered, blue-grey, bloomy
leaves, and greyish white summer flowers.

Rheum palmatum var. *tanguticum*
ORNAMENTAL RHUBARB
☀ ☀ ❄❄❄   ↕ 2.5m (8ft) ↔ 1.8m (6ft)

The striking, huge, toothed and jaggedly
lobed leaves are red-suffused when young.
In summer, branched heads of white, red,
or pink flowers emerge. Superb by water.

Telekia speciosa
TELEKIA
☀ ❄❄❄   ↕ 2m (6ft) ↔ 1.2m (4ft)

This strapping plant forms a large patch of
branching stems, which bear heart-shaped
leaves, and yellow, later brown-centred,
daisy heads in late summer and autumn.

Rheum 'Ace of Hearts'
ORNAMENTAL RHUBARB
☀ ☀ ❄❄❄   ↕ 1.2m (4ft) ↔ 90cm (36in)

The heart-shaped leaves, in impressive
mounds, are red-veined above and purple-
red beneath. Branching stems carry sprays
of pale pinkish white flowers in summer.

Symplocarpus foetidus
SKUNK CABBAGE
☀ ☀ ❄❄❄   ↕ ↔ 60cm (24in)

Curious, hooded, purplish red flowers in
spring are followed by the clump of large,
rather leathery leaves. An excellent bog
plant, it needs plenty of moisture.

Veratrum viride
INDIAN POKE
☀ ☀ ❄❄❄   ↕ 2m (6ft) ↔ 60cm (24in)

The clumps of pleated, rich green leaves,
which appear in spring, are more striking
than the tall, branched spikes of star-
shaped, yellowish green summer flowers.

FOLIAGE EFFECT

123

Perennials with Yellow- or Gold-variegated Foliage

VARIEGATED PERENNIALS and ornamental grasses that have leaves blotched or spotted yellow or gold are often prized for their ability to bring warmth and light to borders dominated by dark green foliage. Many of these perennials also make impressive specimen plants, either grown in containers or in small beds.

Aquilegia vulgaris Vervaeneana Group
GRANNY'S BONNET
☼ ☼ ❄❄❄ ↕90cm (36in) ↔45cm (18in)

The prettily divided leaves are streaked and mottled yellow in this curious form of an old cottage-garden favourite. Spring or summer flowers are white, pink, or purple.

Carex hachijoensis 'Evergold'
SEDGE
☼ ☼ ❄❄❄ ↕30cm (12in) ↔35cm (14in)

This bright little evergreen plant forms a dense, low clump of arching, grass-like, dark green leaves, each with a broad, creamy yellow central stripe. ▽

Convallaria majalis 'Hardwick Hall'
LILY-OF-THE-VALLEY
☼ ❄❄❄ ↕23cm (9in) ↔30cm (12in)

A choice form of a much-loved perennial, slowly developing patches of erect stems. The pairs of attractively veined, bright green leaves have narrow, paler margins.

Cortaderia selloana 'Aureolineata'
PAMPAS GRASS
☼ ❄❄❄ ↕2.2m (7ft) ↔1.5m (5ft)

A variegated form of a familiar, evergreen grass, producing huge mounds of arching, saw-toothed, yellow-margined leaves. Tall flower plumes in summer are a bonus. ▽

Hakonechloa macra 'Aureola'
ORNAMENTAL GRASS
☼ ☼ ❄❄❄ ↕35cm (14in) ↔40cm (16in)

One of the most pleasing of all grasses, with low mounds of yellow, green-striped leaves. In autumn, it bears airy panicles of spikelets and the leaves flush red. ▽

OTHER YELLOW- OR GOLD-VARIEGATED PERENNIALS

Hosta 'Great Expectations'
Hosta 'Kabitan'
Hosta montana 'Aureomarginata', see p.145
Hosta ventricosa 'Aureomaculata'
Mentha x *gracilis* 'Variegata'
Phormium 'Yellow Wave'
Polygonatum odoratum 'Gilt Edge'
Salvia officinalis 'Aurea'
Saxifraga x *urbium* 'Aureopunctata'

Hosta 'Gold Standard'
PLANTAIN LILY
☼ ❄❄❄ ↕65cm (26in) ↔1m (3ft)

This singularly attractive perennial forms clumps of heart-shaped, greenish yellow leaves fading to green margins. Tall stems bear lavender-blue flowers in summer.

Hosta ventricosa 'Variegata'
PLANTAIN LILY
☼ ✳✳✳ ↕ 50cm (20in) ↔ 1m (3ft)

Big, bold clumps of heart-shaped, deep-veined green leaves have irregular yellow margins ageing creamy white. In summer, tall stems bear deep purple flowers. ♔

Iris pallida 'Variegata'
IRIS
☼ ✳✳✳ ↕ 1.2m (4ft) ↔ 60cm (24in)

An effective variegated perennial, with stout clumps of sword-shaped, grey-green or green leaves striped light yellow. In late spring, it bears scented, soft blue flowers.

Miscanthus sinensis 'Zebrinus'
ZEBRA GRASS
☼ ✳✳✳ ↕ ↔ 1.2m (4ft)

This old favourite is especially popular for specimen planting. The bold clumps of slender, cane-like stems bear long, narrow green leaves banded white or pale yellow.

Symphytum 'Goldsmith'
COMFREY
☼ ◐ ✳✳✳ ↕ ↔ 30cm (12in)

Superb ground cover, this creeping plant forms large patches of hairy leaves with irregular gold or cream margins. Blue and white, pink-tinted flowers occur in spring.

Tolmiea menziesii 'Taff's Gold'
PICK-A-BACK PLANT
☼ ◐ ✳✳✳ ↕ 50cm (20in) ↔ 60cm (24in)

Loose clumps of semi-evergreen, prettily lobed, hairy leaves are pale green, spotted and blotched cream and pale yellow. The tiny flowers are of little consequence. ♔

Trifolium pratense 'Susan Smith'
CLOVER
☼ ✳✳✳ ↕ 15cm (6in) ↔ 45cm (18in)

The characteristic clover leaves of this mat-forming perennial have green leaflets that are curiously but attractively netted with golden yellow veins.

Yucca flaccida 'Golden Sword'
YUCCA
☼ ✳✳✳✳ ↕ 1.5m (5ft) ↔ 1m (3ft)

A bold, clump-forming evergreen, bearing stiff, sword-like, blue-green leaves with central yellow bands. Panicles of white bell-flowers emerge in late summer. ♔

OTHER YELLOW-STRIPED GRASSES

Alopecurus pratensis 'Aureovariegatus'
Glyceria maxima 'Variegata'
x *Hibanobambusa tranquilans*
  'Shirobana'
Miscanthus sinensis 'Goldfeder'
Miscanthus sinensis 'Univittatus'
Molinia caerulea 'Variegata'
Phragmites australis 'Variegatus'
Pleioblastus auricomus
Spartina pectinata 'Aureomarginata'

FOLIAGE EFFECT

125

Perennials with White- or Cream-variegated Foliage

IT IS A CURIOUS FACT that there are far more perennials with white- or cream-variegated foliage than with yellow or gold variegation. Patterned with stripes, spots, blotches, marbling, or marginal lines, these leaves provide a useful contrast for plants with green or purple foliage, and can brighten up dark corners or dull combinations in the garden.

Armoracia rusticana 'Variegata'
HORSERADISH
☼ ✳✳✳ ↕ 1m (3ft) ↔ 45cm (18in)

This variegated form of the well-known horseradish has clumps of large, coarse, wholly or partially white leaves. Branched stems of white flowers appear in summer.

Convallaria majalis 'Albostriata'
LILY-OF-THE-VALLEY
☼ ✳✳✳ ↕ 23cm (9in) ↔ 30cm (12in)

A beautiful variety of a favourite garden perennial, with leaves longitudinally striped creamy white. Sprays of nodding, fragrant white bell-flowers open in spring.

Hemerocallis fulva 'Kwanzo Variegata'
DAYLILY
☼ ✳✳✳ ↕ 75cm (30in) ↔ 1.2m (4ft)

Long, strap-shaped, arching leaves with white margins form a bold clump. During summer, double, orange-brown flowers rise above the foliage on strong stems.

Brunnera macrophylla 'Dawson's White'
BRUNNERA
☼ ✳✳✳ ↕ 45cm (18in) ↔ 60cm (24in)

In spring, the low mounds of softly-hairy, heart-shaped leaves, irregularly margined in creamy white, are crowned by sprays of bright blue, forget-me-not flowers.

Euphorbia characias subsp. *wulfenii* 'Burrow Silver'
☼ ✳✳ ↕ ↔ 1.2m (4ft)

Bushy and woody-based, this evergreen has dense, grey-green leaves with creamy margins. Rounded heads of bright yellow-green flowers open in spring and summer.

Hosta 'Shade Fanfare'
PLANTAIN LILY
☼ ✳✳✳ ↕ 45cm (18in) ↔ 60cm (24in)

Excellent for ground cover, the clumps of bold, heart-shaped leaves have irregular cream margins fading to white. Lavender-blue flowers are borne in summer. ♛

Phlox paniculata 'Harlequin'
PERENNIAL PHLOX

☼ ❄❄❄   ↕ 1.2m (4ft) ↔ 1m (3ft)

Robust clumps of erect stems bear leaves boldly margined in creamy white, and are topped by panicles of fragrant, red-purple flowers in summer.

Symphytum × *uplandicum* 'Variegatum'
COMFREY

☼ ☽ ❄❄❄   ↕ 90cm (36in) ↔ 60cm (24in)

A tough, deep-rooted perennial, producing a spectacular clump of white-margined leaves. In summer, striking variegated stems bear blue and pink flowers. 🏆

> ### OTHER PERENNIALS WITH WHITE- OR CREAM-VARIEGATED FOLIAGE
>
> *Astrantia major* 'Sunningdale Variegated'
> *Brunnera macrophylla* 'Hadspen Cream'
> *Iris pallida* 'Argentea Variegata', see p.67
> *Lysimachia punctata* 'Alexander'
> *Mentha suaveolens* 'Variegata'
> *Polemonium caeruleum* 'Brise d'Anjou'
> *Polygonatum* × *hybridum* 'Striatum'
> *Scrophularia auriculata* 'Variegata'

Physostegia virginiana 'Variegata'
PHYSOSTEGIA

☼ ☽ ❄❄❄   ↕ ↔ 45cm (18in)

Both the willow-like leaves and the erect stems of this easily grown perennial are grey-green, variegated white. Magenta-pink flower spikes emerge in late summer.

Myosotis scorpioides 'Maytime'
WATER FORGET-ME-NOT

☼ ❄❄❄   ↕ ↔ 30cm (12in)

Strikingly variegated, this waterside plant forms patches of bold, white-margined leaves. Its sprays of bright blue flowers are produced in early summer.

Pulmonaria 'Roy Davidson'
LUNGWORT

☼ ☽ ❄❄❄   ↕ 30cm (12in) ↔ 60cm (24in)

Clumps of semi-evergreen, roughly-hairy, white-spotted leaves provide good ground cover, with clusters of tubular, blue and red flowers in spring. It will seed around.

Vinca major 'Variegata'
LARGE PERIWINKLE

☼ ☽ ❄❄❄   ↕ 45cm (18in) ↔ 2m (6ft)

This fast-growing, scrambling evergreen forms blankets of striking, paired, creamy white-margined leaves. Pale blue flowers are borne from late winter into spring. 🏆

FOLIAGE EFFECT

127

Perennials with Yellow or Gold Foliage

A SURPRISING NUMBER of garden perennials have produced sports with yellow- or gold-suffused leaves. In some plants, the best foliage effect is achieved in spring; in others the colour is retained through summer. All have an important role in the garden, especially in shaded or dimly lit corners, or as a contrast to greens and purples.

Hosta 'Midas Touch'
PLANTAIN LILY
☼ ☀ ❄❄❄ ↕ 50cm (20in) ↔ 65cm (26in)

There are many golden leaved hostas available, but this is one of the best. It has big, bold, handsomely corrugated foliage and bears lavender-blue summer flowers.

Aquilegia 'Mellow Yellow'
GRANNY'S BONNET
☼ ❄❄❄ ↕ 60cm (24in) ↔ 45cm (18in)

An attractive form of a plant common to cottage gardens, with golden leaves in spring, paling to yellow-green in summer, when white to pale blue flowers appear.

Carex elata 'Aurea'
BOWLES' GOLDEN SEDGE
☼ ☼ ❄❄❄ ↕ 70cm (28in) ↔ 90cm (36in)

Probably the best golden-leaved perennial for waterside sites, this clump-forming sedge has arching, grassy, bright golden leaves. Superb by streams or pools. ♔

Lamium maculatum 'Cannon's Gold'
DEAD NETTLE
☼ ❄❄❄ ↕ 20cm (8in) ↔ 1m (3ft)

The coarsely toothed, semi-evergreen leaves of this plant form a soft yellow carpet in spring and summer. Its mauve-pink flowers emerge in early summer.

Campanula garganica 'Dickson's Gold'
BELLFLOWER
☼ ☼ ❄❄❄ ↕ 5cm (2in) ↔ 30cm (12in)

This cheerful perennial forms a hummock of neat little toothy, kidney-shaped leaves. These turn golden in summer at the same time as small blue flowers are borne.

Centaurea montana 'Gold Bullion'
PERENNIAL CORNFLOWER
☼ ❄❄❄ ↕ 45cm (18in) ↔ 60cm (24in)

A beautiful, golden-leaved version of an old garden favourite. The pronounced leaf colour in spring and early summer is a perfect foil for the large blue cornflowers.

Lysimachia nummularia 'Aurea'
GOLDEN CREEPING JENNY
☼ ☼ ❄❄❄ ↕ 5cm (2in) ↔ indefinite

One of the brightest and most reliable gold-leaved plants, its evergreen carpet of creeping stems turns greenish yellow in shade. Yellow flowers open in summer. ♔

Melissa officinalis 'All Gold'
LEMON BALM
☼ ✳✳✳ ↕ ↔ 60cm (24in)

This bushy perennial produces a dense
clump of lemon-scented, yellow-suffused
stems and leaves. It is especially effective
during spring and early summer.

**Tradescantia × andersoniana
'Blue and Gold'**
☼ ◐ ✳✳✳ ↕ ↔ 45cm (18in)

During summer, rich blue, three-petalled
flowers on erect, fleshy stems contrast
well with this clump-forming perennial's
long, strap-shaped, gold-suffused leaves.

Valeriana phu 'Aurea'
GOLDEN VALERIAN
☼ ◐ ✳✳✳ ↕ 1.5m (5ft) ↔ 60cm (24in)

The prime attraction of this tall, branching
perennial is its gold spring foliage, which
gradually fades to green in summer. Its
small white flowers open in late summer.

Stachys byzantina 'Primrose Heron'
LAMB'S EARS
☼ ✳✳✳ ↕ 45cm (18in) ↔ 60cm (24in)

A vigorous evergreen perennial, forming a
close carpet of velvety, hairy grey stems,
and 'lamb's ear' leaves, which are suffused
yellow in spring and early summer.

Tanacetum vulgare 'Isla Gold'
GOLDEN TANSY
☼ ✳✳✳ ↕ ↔ 90cm (36in)

The golden form of a fine garden stalwart,
with bold clumps of erect stems clothed
in finely divided, aromatic, yellowy leaves.
It bears yellow flowerheads in summer.

OTHER PERENNIALS WITH GOLD FOLIAGE

Acanthus mollis 'Hollard's Gold'
Acorus gramineus 'Ogon'
Carex elata 'Knightshayes'
Deschampsia flexuosa 'Tatra Gold'
Dicentra spectabilis 'Goldheart'
Filipendula ulmaria 'Aurea'
Gaura lindheimeri 'Corrie's Gold'
Hosta 'Golden Prayers'
Hosta 'Sum and Substance', see p.65
Hosta 'Zounds', see p.60
Lamium maculatum 'Golden Nuggets'
Luzula sylvatica 'Aurea'
Melissa officinalis 'Aurea', see p.49
Milium effusum 'Aureum', see p.27
Pleioblastus auricomus
Symphytum ibericum 'Gold in Spring'
Thymus × citriodorus 'Archer's Gold'
Veronica prostrata 'Trehane'

FOLIAGE EFFECT

129

Perennials with Silver or Blue-grey Foliage

PERENNIALS WITH SILVER or blue-grey foliage (often the entire plant is similarly coloured) are particularly valuable in the garden for separating strong-coloured plants, such as those with red, purple, or even green leaves. They can also provide a lovely foil for pastel-coloured flowers, especially those in pink, lavender-purple, pale blue, and yellow. While there is a vast choice of perennials for use in grey or silver borders, they can also make a striking display as specimen plants or grouped together with other contrasting foliage perennials in containers. Most plants with silver leaves prefer a warm, sunny situation.

Cynara cardunculus
CARDOON
☼ ❋❋❋   ↕ 1.5m (5ft) ↔ 1.2m (4ft)

The deeply divided, spiny, silvery grey leaves of this statuesque plant form big, bold clumps. During summer, stout blue flowerheads open on branched stems. ♛

Anaphalis triplinervis 'Sommerschnee'
PEARLY EVERLASTING
☼ ❋❋❋   ↕ 80cm (32in) ↔ 60cm (24in)

A German selection of a reliable perennial. The clumps of grey stems bear leaves that are white-woolly beneath, and dense white flower clusters in late summer. ♛

Cerastium tomentosum
SNOW-IN-SUMMER
☼ ❋❋❋   ↕ 8cm (3in) ↔ 1.5m (5ft)

One of the best grey ground-cover plants for walls and sunny banks. White flowers pepper the carpet of evergreen, downy leaves from late spring into summer.

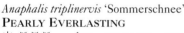

Artemisia ludoviciana var. *albula*
ARTEMISIA
☼ ❋❋❋   ↕ 1.2m (4ft) ↔ 60cm (24in)

The erect clumps of slender, woolly stems bear willow-like, sharp-toothed, aromatic, white-woolly leaves, and dense white flower clusters in summer and autumn.

Crambe maritima
SEA KALE
☼ ❋❋❋   ↕ 75cm (30in) ↔ 60cm (24in)

This distinctive, bold, mound-forming plant has large, deep-lobed, twisted, blue-green, bloomy leaves, and branched heads of small white flowers in early summer.

Dicentra 'Langtrees'
DICENTRA
☼ ❋❋❋   ↕ 30cm (12in) ↔ 45cm (18in)

A charming plant, with mounds of ferny, silvery blue leaves, topped in late spring and early summer by nodding clusters of white flowers. Forms patches in time. ♛

Galanthus caucasicus of gardens
SNOWDROP
☼ ☼ ✳✳✳   ↕15cm (6in) ↔ 8cm (3in)

Eventually forming large colonies, this vigorous, bold snowdrop has broad, blue-green leaves, and nodding white flowers with green-marked inner segments. ♔

EVERGREEN PERENNIALS WITH SILVER OR BLUE-GREY FOLIAGE

Artemisia 'Powis Castle', see p.20
Astelia chathamica
Celmisia spectabilis
Euphorbia nicaeensis, see p.76
Festuca glauca 'Blaufuchs', see p.138
Heuchera 'Pewter Moon'
Kniphofia caulescens, see p.114
Stachys byzantina 'Big Ears'
Tanacetum argenteum
Yucca glauca

Hosta 'Blue Moon'
PLANTAIN LILY
☼ ✳✳✳   ↕10cm (4in) ↔ 30cm (12in)

Slow-growing, but worth waiting for, with its attractive clump of bloomy, blue-green, heart-shaped leaves, and dense racemes of mauve-grey flowers borne in summer.

HERBACEOUS PERENNIALS WITH SILVER OR BLUE-GREY FOLIAGE

Aquilegia vulgaris 'Nivea'
Cynara scolymus 'Glauca'
Hosta 'Hadspen Blue', see p.67
Iris pallida
Lychnis flos-jovis
Macleaya cordata
Rudbeckia maxima
Sanguisorba obtusa
Thalictrum flavum subsp. *glaucum*, see p.29

Helictotrichon sempervirens
BLUE OAT GRASS
☼ ✳✳✳   ↕1.5m (5ft) ↔ 60cm (24in)

A striking, evergreen grass, forming a bold clump of stiff, narrow, grey-blue leaves. A sheaf of erect stems bears panicles of tiny spikelets above the leaves in summer. ♔

Lysimachia ephemerum
LOOSESTRIFE
☼ ☼ ✳✳✳   ↕1m (3ft) ↔ 30cm (12in)

The erect stems of this fine perennial are densely clothed in willowy, bloomy, sea-green leaves and sport slender spires of small white flowers in summer.

Verbascum olympicum
MULLEIN
☼ ✳✳✳   ↕2m (6ft) ↔ 60cm (24in)

This stately, silvery, white-woolly biennial or perennial has a rosette of overwintering leaves, and tall, branched stems that bear dense spikes of yellow flowers in summer.

FOLIAGE EFFECT

131

Perennials with Purple, Red, or Bronze Foliage

WHEN USED SELECTIVELY in garden plantings, perennials with unusual deep purple, bronze, or red foliage can provide a striking contrast among plants with lighter green, grey, or even yellow leaves. In some perennials, like *Cimicifuga simplex* 'Brunette', the colour is long-lasting or even permanent, while in others it is mainly a spring display created by newly emerging foliage and stems. Sometimes the rich leaf colour is also attractively overlaid by a lovely pale bloom, as is the case in several sedums.

Artemisia lactiflora 'Guizhou'
CHINESE MUGWORT

☼ ✳✳✳   ↕ 1.5m (5ft) ↔ 1m (3ft)

A vigorous perennial, producing clumps of branching, dark purple-flushed stems and deeply cut leaves. Sprays of tiny white flowers open from summer into autumn.

EVERGREEN PERENNIALS WITH PURPLE, RED, OR BRONZE LEAVES
Ajuga reptans 'Atropurpurea'
Ajuga reptans 'Braunherz'
Euphorbia amygdaloides 'Purpurea'
Phormium 'Maori Chief'
Phormium tenax 'Purpureum'
Salvia officinalis 'Purpurascens'
Sedum spathulifolium 'Atropurpureum'
Sempervivum 'Othello'
Uncinia rubra
Veronica peduncularis 'Georgia Blue'

Heuchera 'Rachel'
CORAL FLOWER

☼ ☼ ✳✳✳   ↕ 60cm (24in) ↔ 45cm (18in)

This striking plant forms a low clump of large, crinkled and lobed, shiny, bronze-purple leaves, bright purple beneath. Tiny off-white summer flowers open in sprays.

Cimicifuga simplex 'Brunette'
BUGBANE

☼ ✳✳✳   ↕ 1.2m (4ft) ↔ 60cm (24in)

This superb perennial has clumps of large, divided, purplish brown leaves. Arching stems bear tall racemes of purple-tinted white flowers above the foliage in autumn.

Euphorbia dulcis 'Chameleon'
SPURGE

☼ ☼ ✳✳✳   ↕ ↔ 30cm (12in)

The branching, purplish stems bear small red-purple leaves, which colour richly in autumn. Clouds of purple-tinted flowers are borne in summer. It will seed around.

Imperata cylindrica 'Rubra'
IMPERATA

☼ ☼ ✳✳   ↕ 40cm (16in) ↔ 30cm (12in

An attractive grass with erect, leafy shoots and long green leaves that soon turn deep blood-red from the tips down. In summer, it bears sprays of silver-white spikelets.

Ophiopogon planiscapus 'Nigrescens'
LILYTURF
☼☀ ❆❆❆ ↕ 20cm (8in) ↔ 30cm (12in)

Ideal for ground cover, the low, evergreen
tufts of narrow, leathery, blackish purple
leaves form patches in time. It has slender
purple-white flower sprays in summer. ♈

Phormium 'Dazzler'
NEW ZEALAND FLAX
☼ ❆❆❆ ↕ 1m (3ft) ↔ 1.2m (4ft)

This flax has stout clumps of evergreen,
arching, strap-shaped, leathery leaves,
impressively striped red, orange, and pink
on a bronze-purple background.

Ranunculus ficaria 'Brazen Hussy'
LESSER CELANDINE
☼·☀ ❆❆❆ ↕ 5cm (2in) ↔ 15cm (6in)

The small rosettes or patches of long-
stalked, heart-shaped, glossy, chocolate-
brown leaves are an ideal backing for the
shining, golden yellow flowers in spring.

Rodgersia podophylla
RODGERSIA
☼·☀ ❆❆❆ ↕ 1.5m (5ft) ↔ 1.8m (6ft)

Bronze-red when young, the large clumps
of long-stalked, deeply divided and lobed
leaves colour red again in autumn. White
flower plumes are borne in summer. ♈

**HERBACEOUS PERENNIALS WITH
PURPLE, RED, OR BRONZE LEAVES**

Anthriscus sylvestris 'Ravenswing'
Clematis recta 'Purpurea'
Foeniculum vulgare 'Purpureum',
  see p.119
Heuchera micrantha var. *diversifolia*
  'Palace Purple'
Lobelia 'Queen Victoria'
Penstemon digitalis 'Husker Red'
Sedum telephium subsp. *maximum*
  'Atropurpureum'

Sedum 'Matrona'
ICE PLANT
☼ ❆❆❆ ↕ 60cm (24in) ↔ 30cm (12in)

From late summer into autumn, flattened
heads of starry pink flowers rise on stout,
fleshy, purple-red stems above the robust
clumps of fleshy, bloomy purple leaves.

Sedum 'Sunset Cloud'
ICE PLANT
☼ ❆❆❆ ↕ 25cm (10in) ↔ 45cm (18in)

One of the best of the low-growing purple
sedums, it has fleshy, trailing or lax stems,
bloomy foliage, and flattened pink flowerheads in late summer and autumn.

Perennials with Richly Tinted Autumn Foliage

ALL TOO OFTEN when we think of autumn colour in the garden we look to woody, deciduous plants, like maples or sumachs, ignoring the merits of the many herbaceous perennials, like those below, which also produce a burst of bright colour before winter arrives.

OTHER PERENNIALS WITH RICHLY TINTED AUTUMN FOLIAGE

Agapanthus 'Loch Hope', see p.64
Aruncus aethusifolius, see p.119
Ceratostigma plumbaginoides, see p.44
Darmera peltata, see p.60
Euphorbia griffithii 'Fireglow', see p.84
Geranium macrorrhizum, see p.83
Hosta fortunei
Imperata cylindrica 'Rubra', see p.132
Miscanthus sinensis 'Flammemeer'
Osmunda regalis, see p.61

Geranium wlassovianum
CRANESBILL
☼ ◑ ❄❄❄   ↕ ↔ 60cm (24in)

The clumps of long-stalked, deeply lobed, softly-downy and velvety leaves emerge pinkish bronze in spring, then turn a rich red, with purple-bronze tints, in autumn.

Schizachyrium scoparium
LITTLE BLUESTEM
☼ ❄❄❄   ↕ 1m (3ft) ↔ 30cm (12in)

The dense tufts of arching, greyish green leaves and upright stems turn purple to orange-red in autumn. Narrow heads of whiskery spikelets are borne in summer.

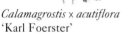

Calamagrostis x *acutiflora*
'Karl Foerster'
☼ ◑ ❄❄❄   ↕ 1.8m (6ft) ↔ 60cm (24in)

This striking, clump-forming ornamental grass has stiffly erect stems and arching leaves. The pinky bronze spikelets turn a warm buff or pale brown in autumn.

Darmera peltata 'Nana'
UMBRELLA PLANT
☼ ◑ ❄❄❄   ↕ 35cm (14in) ↔ 60cm (24in)

A dwarf form of the umbrella plant, with long-stalked, rounded leaves that turn red or orange-copper in autumn. Leafless stems bear clusters of pink spring flowers.

Pennisetum setaceum 'Rubrum'
FOUNTAIN GRASS
☼ ❄❄   ↕ 1m (3ft) ↔ 60cm (24in)

Spectacular and strong-growing, this grass forms a clump of erect, rich purple stems and leaves. The arching or pendent pink, slender spikes fade to pink-buff or white.

Sedum aizoon
STONECROP
☼ ❄❄❄   ↕ ↔ 45cm (18in)

In autumn, the clumps of erect, reddish stems and fleshy, coarsely toothed leaves turn red or orange-red. Flattened heads of yellow star-flowers open in summer.

Perennials with Decorative Winter Foliage

IF PERENNIALS WITH RICHLY TINTED FOLIAGE in autumn are useful in the garden, then those with decorative foliage in winter are invaluable. When many plants have either died down or lost their leaves, these perennials will brighten up borders and beds with their yellow- or white-variegated, red-suffused, silver-hairy, or beautifully marbled leaves.

Epimedium × *rubrum*
EPIMEDIUM
☼ ☼ ✳✳✳   ↕ ↔ 30cm (12in)

Red-flushed when young, the clumps of much-divided leaves become red-tinted in autumn, and remain throughout winter. Spring flowers are crimson and yellow. ♛

Celmisia semicordata
NEW ZEALAND DAISY   ☼ ☼
✳✳✳✳^PH   ↕ 50cm (20in) ↔ 30cm (12in)

Grey-green above and silvery beneath, the sword-shaped, silky-hairy leaves form a bold rosette or clump. Grey-downy stems bear large daisy-heads in summer.

Arum italicum 'Marmoratum'
ARUM
☼ ✳✳✳   ↕ 30cm (12in) ↔ 25cm (10in)

One of the most reliable and eye-catching winter foliage plants, with arrow-shaped, pale-veined, shiny leaves. Greenish white flowers are borne in early spring. ♛

> **OTHER PERENNIALS WITH DECORATIVE WINTER FOLIAGE**
>
> *Asplenium scolopendrium* 'Crispum', see p.141
> *Euphorbia characias* subsp. *wulfenii* 'Purple and Gold'
> *Galax urceolata*
> *Helleborus argutifolius*, see p.114
> *Phormium* 'Sundowner'
> *Pulmonaria saccharata* 'Leopard', see p.115
> *Tellima grandiflora* 'Purpurea'

Bergenia 'Ballawley'
ELEPHANT'S EAR
☼ ☼ ✳✳✳   ↕ 60cm (24in) ↔ 45cm (18in)

The low clumps of leathery, glossy green leaves turn rich bronze-purple or purplish red in winter. In spring, upright red stems carry clusters of crimson bell-flowers.

Cyclamen coum Pewter Group
HARDY CYCLAMEN
☼ ✳✳✳   ↕ 8cm (3in) ↔ 10cm (4in)

A beautiful selection of a popular, winter-flowering cyclamen, with kidney-shaped, silvered, often dark-green-centred leaves. Reddish pink flowers add to its charm. ♛

Sasa veitchii
SASA
☼ ☼ ☼ ✳✳✳   ↕ 1.5m (5ft) ↔ indefinite

This vigorous, creeping bamboo has bold, evergreen leaves that wither at the edges in autumn, giving them decorative white margins for winter. It needs lots of space.

SPECIALIST PLANTS

CERTAIN PERENNIALS are now some of the most enthusiastically collected garden plants. Valued for their foliage, flowers, or form, their increasing availability is making it easier than ever to establish a specialist collection.

Polystichum munitum
for moisture
or shade

△ HELLEBORES *Excellent for ground cover,* Helleborus x hybridus *seedlings are some of the most desirable perennials.*

Imagine a garden filled with 100 different hardy geraniums, or 50 assorted peonies, or even a multitude of hardy ferns. In fact, there are many such gardens, and they are on the increase as the fashion for collecting members of a single genus or family continues to catch gardeners' imaginations. Although collecting has appealed to plantsmen and women in Europe for the last 400 years at least, and for many centuries more in China and Japan, enthusiasm for specialist perennials has recently greatly increased.

The perennials in this section are among the most sought after plants. Some, such as snowdrops and geraniums, have long been popular, with numerous varieties already available, and many more introduced each year. Others, like ornamental grasses, which have the combined attraction of elegant habit, foliage, and seed heads, and hellebores and epimediums, have been "discovered" more recently, but are now avidly collected.

MIX AND MATCH

While the search for as many varieties of a particular perennial as possible can be a mixture of fun and adventure, the entire garden does not have to be filled with just one plant and its variations. If you are selective, choosing only the best varieties or those that appeal to you, it is possible to combine a collection of specialist perennials with other garden plants to provide varied, year-round appeal.

ESTABLISHING A COLLECTION

So many different perennials are available that it is easy to establish a collection to suit the size and situation of your garden. Sedums or saxifrages, for example, can be grown in a small urban backyard using troughs or containers, and if your chosen plants are large shrubs or bush roses, ground-cover plants such as hardy geraniums can be grown beneath them. With the right conditions, several collections can be established together: hardy ferns, snowdrops, pulmonarias, and epimediums will all thrive in each other's company.

△ PEONIES *Famed for their foliage and flowers, classics like* Paeonia x smouthii *will make a striking show in the garden.*

◁ GERANIUMS *Justifiably popular and very easy to grow, geraniums are perfect for ground cover, or for borders and beds.*

▷ MIXED GRASSES *When planted for contrasting effect, as here, ornamental grasses can make a spectacular collection.*

Small Grasses and Sedges

L ONG NEGLECTED, perennial grasses and sedges are now being rediscovered and increasingly cultivated for their ornamental value. Ideal for smaller gardens, those suggested below will make a striking addition to a border, or good specimen plants.

Festuca glauca 'Blaufuchs'
BLUE FESCUE
☼ ❄❄❄ ↕ 30cm (12in) ↔ 25cm (10in)

Good for contrast, this is one of the best small, blue-leaved grasses. Its name, 'Blue Fox', aptly describes the dense tufts of narrow, bright blue leaves and stiff shoots.

Carex muskingumensis
PALM SEDGE
☼ ❄❄❄ ↕ 60cm (24in) ↔ 45cm (18in)

With its loosely tufted habit, erect, leafy shoots, and horizontally spreading leaves, this sedge resembles a miniature cabbage palm (*Cordyline australis*) or a bamboo.

> **OTHER SMALL GRASSES AND SEDGES**
>
> *Bouteloua gracilis*
> *Carex hachijoensis* 'Evergold', see p.124
> *Festuca glauca* 'Golden Toupee'
> *Imperata cylindrica* 'Rubra', see p.132
> *Miscanthus sinensis* 'Sioux'
> *Stipa tenuissima*, see p.71

Deschampsia cespitosa 'Goldschleier'
TUFTED HAIR GRASS
☼ ☼ ❄❄❄❄ PH ▼ ↕↔ 1m (3ft)

During summer, slender shoots bearing showers of tiny green spikelets, maturing to bright silvery yellow, rise above the bold clumps of narrow, evergreen leaves.

Pennisetum orientale
FOUNTAIN GRASS
☼ ❄❄ ↕ 60cm (24in) ↔ 75cm (30in)

A superb specimen plant with a dense, neat mound of narrow leaves, and arching shoots bearing spikes of soft, long-bristled, pink-tinted spikelets in summer. ♔

Carex siderosticha 'Variegata'
SEDGE
☼ ☼ ❄❄❄ ↕ 30cm (12in) ↔ 40cm (16in)

One of the most ornamental sedges, with a creeping habit useful for ground cover. Its arching, strap-shaped, white-margined leaves form a low, dense hummock.

Elymus magellanicus
ELYMUS
☼ ❄❄❄ ↕ 60cm (24in) ↔ 30cm (12in)

Both the tufts of long, slender leaves, and the shoots that carry narrow flower-spikes in summer, are an intense, almost electric blue. Excellent as a specimen plant.

Stipa tenuifolia
STIPA
☼ ❄❄❄ ↕ 60cm (24in) ↔ 75cm (30in)

This graceful grass has dense clumps of long, slender, bright green leaves, and bears arching, feathery plumes in summer. Ideal for associating with other perennials.

Large Ornamental Grasses

GROWN AS SPECIMENS IN A LAWN, or in a bed underplanted with smaller perennials, these bold grasses can create a grand spectacle, especially in late summer or autumn when in flower. They are all easy to cultivate and can be planted singly or in groups for a more immediate effect.

Cortaderia selloana 'Sunningdale Silver'

☼ ❄❄❄   ↕ 3m (10ft) ↔ 2.5m (8ft)

A big, bold, evergreen, pampas grass with sturdy stems bearing large, silvery white plumes that last well into winter. This is a popular and well-proven variety. ♔

OTHER LARGE GRASSES

Arundo donax 'Macrophylla', see p.116
Cortaderia selloana 'Rendatleri',
   see p.22
Miscanthus sacchariflorus
Miscanthus sinensis 'Silberfeder'
Miscanthus sinensis 'Zebrinus', see p.125
Stipa gigantea

Calamagrostis brachytricha
REED GRASS

☼ ☼ ❄❄❄   ↕ 1.2m (4ft) ↔ 1m (3ft)

Dense clumps of erect shoots bear narrow heads of purplish spikelets in late summer or autumn. Excellent for winter effect, the spikelets later turn a warm brown.

Chionochloa conspicua
PLUMED TUSSOCK GRASS

☼ ❄❄   ↕ 2m (6ft) ↔ 1m (3ft)

Graceful, branched heads of creamy white spikelets, maturing pale silver-brown, rise on tall shoots in summer above the clump of evergreen, reddish brown-tinted leaves.

Cortaderia richardii
TOE TOE

☼ ❄❄❄   ↕ 3m (10ft) ↔ 2m (6ft)

During summer, tall shoots extend from the mound of arching, evergreen leaves to flaunt graceful, drooping, creamy white, shaggy plumes, which persist into winter.

Miscanthus sinensis 'Cabaret'
MISCANTHUS

☼ ❄❄❄   ↕ 1.8m (6ft) ↔ 1.2m (4ft)

Conspicuous white stripes line the leaves of this attractive, clump-forming grass. In autumn, it bears feathery flowerheads that rise above the foliage.

Ferns for Moisture or Shade

O F ALL NON-FLOWERING PERENNIALS, ferns are easily the most garden-worthy, offering an exciting variety of shapes and heights for use as specimen plants or in bold groupings. Most of the following ferns are of medium to large size, and will thrive given humus-rich soil, moisture, and shade.

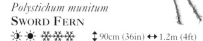

Polystichum munitum
SWORD FERN
☼ ☀ ✳✳✳ ↕ 90cm (36in) ↔ 1.2m (4ft)

Once it is established, this luxuriant fern can transform an otherwise dull corner or border. Its laddered, evergreen fronds will form a large, handsome clump.

Asplenium scolopendrium
HART'S TONGUE FERN
☼ ☀ ✳✳✳ ↕ ↔ 60cm (24in)

This bold fern is easily recognized by its long, leathery, strap-shaped, evergreen fronds, marked beneath with stripes of brown spores. Fond of alkaline soil. ♕

Dryopteris erythrosora
JAPANESE RED SHIELD FERN
☼ ☀ ✳✳✳ ↕ ↔ 60cm (24in)

One of the most colourful of hardy ferns, its coppery red young fronds in spring and summer contrast with the shiny, dark green, overwintering, mature fronds. ♕

OTHER FERNS FOR MOISTURE OR SHADE

Dryopteris affinis 'Cristata The King'
Dryopteris goldieana
Dryopteris filix-mas
Matteuccia struthiopteris, see p.65
Osmunda cinnamomea
Osmunda regalis, see p.61
Polystichum acrostichoides
Polystichum braunii

Polystichum polyblepharum
JAPANESE TASSEL FERN
☼ ☀ ✳✳✳ ↕ 60cm (24in) ↔ 90cm (36in)

The distinctive shuttlecock of prickle-toothed, much-divided fronds is covered at first with golden hairs. It is particularly effective when planted with other ferns.

Athyrium filix-femina
LADY FERN
☼ ✳✳✳ ↕ 1.2m (4ft) ↔ 60cm (24in)

Finely divided, herbaceous, light green fronds form a graceful shuttlecock, with a green or red-brown central stalk. It is especially good for waterside sites. ♕

Dryopteris wallichiana
WALLICH'S WOOD FERN
☼ ✳✳✳ ↕ 90cm (36in) ↔ 75cm (30in)

The erect fronds of this lovely fern form a big, semi-evergreen shuttlecock and have dark-scaly stalks. Its fronds grow taller if rich soil and shelter are provided. ♕

Polystichum setiferum
SOFT SHIELD FERN
☼ ☀ ✳✳✳ ↕ 1.2m (4ft) ↔ 90cm (36in)

This graceful and beautiful fern develops a large, loose shuttlecock of evergreen, finely divided, dark green fronds. It will thrive on a shady bank or ditch. ♕

Ferns for Walls and Crevices

FERNS THAT PREFER growing in the crevices of rocks and cliffs in the wild are mostly small to very small in size. They can be established in similar situations in the garden, in damp stone walls where space between the stones allows, or they may be used as charming container or trough plants.

Asplenium trichomanes
MAIDENHAIR SPLEENWORT
☼ ☼ ☼ ✳✳✳✳   ↕ 15cm (6in) ↔ 20cm (8in)

Delicate-looking but tough, this little fern produces an evergreen rosette of slender, black-stalked fronds with neatly paired divisions. It prefers alkaline conditions.

Asplenium adiantum-nigrum
BLACK SPLEENWORT
☼ ☼ ✳✳✳   ↕ 15cm (6in) ↔ 20cm (8in)

A tough little evergreen fern with wiry black stalks and triangular, much-divided, leathery, shiny green fronds. It thrives in alkaline soils.

Asplenium ceterach
RUSTY-BACK FERN
☼ ☼ ✳✳✳   ↕ 12.5cm (5in) ↔ 25cm (10in)

This is quite unlike any other hardy fern in its tuffet of scaly-backed, deeply lobed, strap-shaped, evergreen fronds, which curl in times of drought, recovering after rain.

OTHER FERNS FOR WALLS AND CREVICES

Adiantum capillus-veneris
Asplenium viride
Cheilanthes feei
Cheilanthes tomentosa
Cystopteris fragilis
Pellaea atropurpurea
Polypodium vulgare 'Cornubiense', see p.115

Asplenium ruta-muraria
WALL RUE
☼ ☼ ☼ ✳✳✳✳   ↕ 10cm (4in) ↔ 12.5cm (5in)

Often found with *A. trichomanes* in the wild, this wall rue forms dense colonies of small, much-divided, leathery, evergreen fronds. It is fond of alkaline conditions.

Asplenium scolopendrium 'Crispum'
HART'S TONGUE FERN
☼ ☼ ✳✳✳✳   ↕ 50cm (20in) ↔ 60cm (24in)

The strap-shaped, wavy-margined, shiny fronds of this curiously attractive, evergreen fern gradually form a bold clump. Also ideal for the front of a shady border.

Polypodium cambricum
Pulcherrimum Group
☼ ☼ ✳✳✳   ↕ 45cm (18in) ↔ 60cm (24in)

The decorative, regularly and deeply divided, triangular to lance-shaped fronds have crested tips, and emerge in summer, staying fresh and green until late winter.

Woodsia polystichoides
HOLLY FERN WOODSIA
☼ ✳✳✳   ↕ 20cm (8in) ↔ 25cm (10in)

One of the prettiest ferns for walls or rock crevices, producing small clumps of lance-shaped, deeply divided, pale green fronds. It may be damaged by late spring frosts.

Tall, Vigorous Bamboos

THE VIGOUR, LUSH INFORMALITY, and glossy, ever-moving, evergreen foliage of these tall-growing bamboos make them ideal for screening, especially on moist, well-drained soils in sheltered sites. Superb for large gardens or woodland, their growth can be curbed in smaller sites using containers.

Semiarundinaria fastuosa
NARIHIRA BAMBOO
☼ ☀ ❄❄❄   ↕ 5m (15ft) ↔ 4m (12ft)

This stately, erect bamboo has purple-brown-striped canes, with dense sprays of foliage. Clump-forming in cool climates, it spreads extensively in warmer areas. ♛

OTHER TALL, VIGOROUS BAMBOOS
Phyllostachys aurea
Phyllostachys aureosulcata
Phyllostachys aureosulcata 'Spectabilis'
Phyllostachys edulis
Phyllostachys nigra 'Boryana'
Phyllostachys vivax 'Aureocaulis'
Pleioblastus simonii
Semiarundinaria yashadake
Yushania maculata

Chimonobambusa quadrangularis
SQUARE-STEMMED BAMBOO
☼ ❄❄   ↕ 5m (16ft) ↔ indefinite

The older canes of this very fast-growing bamboo are peculiarly four-angled, and mature from green to brown. They carry large sprays of arching, shiny green leaves.

Pseudosasa japonica
METAKE
☼ ☀ ❄❄❄   ↕ 6m (20ft) ↔ indefinite

A handsome bamboo, commonly grown for screening. The heavy mass of striking green foliage forces the dense stands of green canes to arch at the tips in maturity.

Phyllostachys viridiglaucescens
PHYLLOSTACHYS
☼ ☀ ❄❄❄   ↕ 5m (16ft) ↔ indefinite

Like all *Phyllostachys* species, it produces pairs of branches from the cane joints. Large stands of green canes arch widely under the weight of its lush, glossy foliage.

Qiongzhuea tumidinoda
QIONGZU CANE
☀ ❄❄❄   ↕ 5m (15ft) ↔ indefinite

Recently introduced from China, this bamboo with swollen cane joints is famous as a source of walking sticks. The sprays of narrow leaves turn yellowy in full sun.

Yushania anceps
ANCEPS BAMBOO
☼ ☀ ❄❄❄   ↕ 4m (12ft) ↔ indefinite

The most popular bamboo for screening, forming a dense thicket of slender, glossy canes, with arching to pendent branches thickly clothed in fresh green foliage. ♛

Clump-forming Bamboos

THERE ARE FEW MORE ELEGANT and impressive evergreen perennials than those bamboos that slowly increase to form single clumps of canes. They are best displayed as specimens in a sheltered lawn, bed, or woodland glade, and are lovely by water as long as they are not planted in wet soil.

OTHER CLUMP-FORMING BAMBOOS
Chusquea culeou 'Tenuis'
Fargesia denudata
Fargesia robusta
Himalayacalamus falconeri 'Damarapa'
Thamnocalamus crassinodus 'Kew Beauty'
Thamnocalamus spathiflorus

Chusquea culeou
FOXTAIL BAMBOO
☼ ☀ ❄❄❄   ↕ 6m (20ft) ↔ 2.5m (8ft)

The densely packed, yellowish or green canes form an impressive, vase-shaped clump, and look like fox-tails with their branch clusters crowded at each joint. 🏆

Fargesia murieliae
UMBRELLA BAMBOO
☼ ❄❄❄   ↕ 4m (12ft) ↔ 3m (10ft)

A popular specimen plant, forming a vase-shaped clump of arching, bloomy white canes, ageing through green to yellowish green, with plumes of slender leaves. 🏆

Semiarundinaria yamadorii
SEMIARUNDINARIA
☼ ☀ ❄❄❄   ↕ 3m (10ft) ↔ 2m (6ft)

Well-furnished with a mass of handsome, dense green foliage, this is a bamboo of real character and value. Its tall, narrow green canes form a dense, upright clump.

Fargesia nitida
FOUNTAIN BAMBOO
☼ ☀ ❄❄❄   ↕ 5m (15ft) ↔ 3m (10ft)

This aptly named bamboo has a bold, dense clump of slender, arching, purplish canes, which mature to yellow-green and bear showers of narrow leaves. 🏆

Thamnocalamus tessellatus
ZULU BAMBOO
☼ ☀ ❄❄❄   ↕ 4m (12ft) ↔ 2m (6ft)

Conspicuous, papery white sheaths clothe the tall canes of this dense, clump-forming bamboo, giving them a banded effect. It was once used to make Zulu shields.

Geraniums for Collectors

HARDY GERANIUMS, or cranesbills as they are known, are among the most popular of all perennials. This is partly because of their many uses in the garden, and partly due to their great variety of habit, foliage, and flowers. No garden should be without at least a few of the following.

OTHER GERANIUMS FOR COLLECTORS

Geranium 'Brookside', see p.27
Geranium clarkei 'Kashmir Pink'
Geranium maculatum f. *albiflorum*
Geranium maderense
Geranium x *riversleaianum* 'Russell Prichard', see p.100
Geranium sinense
Geranium wlassovianum, see p.134

Geranium 'Salome'
CRANESBILL
☼ ☀ ❅❅❅   ‡ 30cm (12in) ↔ 2m (6ft)

The faintly marbled leaves of this low-grower are suffused yellow when young. Dusky violet-pink flowers, with dark veins and eyes, appear from summer to autumn.

Geranium himalayense 'Plenum'
CRANESBILL
☼ ☀ ❅❅❅   ‡ 25cm (10in) ↔ 60cm (24in)

Also known as 'Birch Double', this pretty cranesbill is ideal for the front of a border. It has neatly divided leaves, and loosely double, old-fashioned blooms in summer.

Geranium 'Nimbus'
CRANESBILL
☼ ☀ ❅❅❅   ‡ 40cm (16in) ↔ 60cm (24in)

This low-grower spreads by underground, creeping stems to form a mound of prettily divided leaves, which are yellowish when young. It has purple-pink summer flowers.

Geranium sylvaticum 'Amy Doncaster'
WOOD CRANESBILL
☼ ☀ ❅❅❅   ‡ 70cm (28in) ↔ 50cm (18in)

In summer, this lovely form of the wood cranesbill bears white-eyed, deep purple-blue flowers. It commemorates the plantswoman who first selected it in her garden.

Geranium kishtvariense
CRANESBILL
☼ ☀ ❅❅❅   ‡ 30cm (12in) ↔ 60cm (24in)

Creeping, underground stems form a low patch of wrinkled, deeply lobed leaves. Brilliant pinkish purple, finely lined flowers appear in summer and autumn.

Geranium phaeum 'Lily Lovell'
MOURNING WIDOW
☼ ☀ ❅❅❅   ‡ 80cm (32in) ↔ 45cm (18in)

A charming form of the mourning widow cranesbill, with attractively lobed, light green leaves, and showers of rich mauve, white-eyed flowers during summer.

Geranium wallichianum
CRANESBILL
☼ ☀ ❅❅❅   ‡ 30cm (12in) ↔ 90cm (36in)

The attractively lined, lilac-purple flowers of this carpeting cranesbill are borne over a long period from summer into autumn. Its marbled leaves are shallowly lobed.

Hostas for Collectors

THE ALREADY BEWILDERING NUMBER of hostas increases each year, with new variations in leaf shape, size, texture, and colour, and the bonus of attractive flowers. The favourites selected here are ideal for planting singly, or in groups or drifts. They are also handsome container plants for paved areas.

Hosta lancifolia
PLANTAIN LILY
☀ ☀ ❄❄❄ ↕ 45cm (18in) ↔ 75cm (30in)

Long grown in gardens, this reliable hosta forms a loose clump of narrow, glossy, dark green leaves, good for ground cover. It has racemes of purple flowers in summer. ♛

Hosta gracillima
PLANTAIN LILY
☀ ☀ ❄❄❄ ↕ 5cm (2in) ↔ 18cm (7in)

Charming for containers, rock gardens, or walls, this tiny hosta's spreading, narrow leaves have wavy margins. It bears slender spires of pinkish violet flowers in autumn.

OTHER HOSTAS FOR COLLECTORS
Hosta fluctuans 'Sagae'
Hosta 'Great Expectations'
Hosta 'King Michael'
Hosta 'Northern Halo'
Hosta opipara
Hosta plantaginea 'Aphrodite'
Hosta 'Snowden'
Hosta 'Summer Fragrance'
Hosta 'Zounds', see p.60

Hosta 'Buckshaw Blue'
PLANTAIN LILY
☀ ☀ ❄❄❄ ↕ 35cm (14in) ↔ 60cm (24in)

The heart-shaped, slightly "dished" leaves are boldly veined and beautifully bloomy, forming a striking clump. Nodding flowers open in short-stalked racemes in summer.

Hosta montana 'Aureomarginata'
PLANTAIN LILY
☀ ☀ ❄❄❄ ↕ 70cm (28in) ↔ 90cm (36in)

Slow to establish but worth the wait, this is a superb specimen plant for containers or borders. It has long-stalked, large, shiny leaves, irregularly margined in bright gold.

Hosta 'Golden Tiara'
PLANTAIN LILY
☀ ☀ ❄❄❄ ↕ 30cm (12in) ↔ 50cm (20in)

One of the best small hostas, it forms a compact clump of heart-shaped, yellowy-margined leaves. It has tall racemes of lavender-purple flowers in summer. ♛

Hosta hypoleuca
PLANTAIN LILY
☀ ☀ ❄❄❄ ↕ 45cm (18in) ↔ 90cm (36in)

This attractive species has large, pale green leaves, with a grey bloom above and striking, mealy-white undersides. It bears pale mauve to white flowers in summer.

Hosta tokudama
PLANTAIN LILY
☀ ☀ ❄❄❄ ↕ 35cm (14in) ↔ 90cm (36in)

Beautiful but slow-growing, this hosta has pale mauve to white flowers in summer, and forms a compact clump of rounded to heart-shaped, corrugated, glaucous leaves.

Snowdrops for Collectors

IF YOU ARE THRILLED BY THE SIGHT of a drift of common snowdrops in the late winter garden or in woodland, then prepare for a pleasant surprise. There are dozens of lesser known varieties of snowdrop, each with its own particular charm and characteristics, and most are very easy to cultivate.

Galanthus nivalis 'Scharlockii'
SNOWDROP
☀ ❄❄❄ ↕ ↔ 10cm (4in)

This curious form of the common snowdrop has nodding, green-tipped flowers, with spathes split into two segments that stand above the blooms like rabbit's ears.

Galanthus 'Augustus'
SNOWDROP
☀ ❄❄❄ ↕ 15cm (6in) ↔ 8cm (3in)

This robust snowdrop has relatively wide, silver-channelled leaves, and distinctly rounded, large flowers with green-tipped inner segments. It forms colonies in time.

> **OTHER SNOWDROPS FOR COLLECTORS**
>
> *Galanthus* 'Barbara's Double'
> *Galanthus* 'Benhall Beauty'
> *Galanthus caucasicus* 'Comet'
> *Galanthus* 'Merlin'
> *Galanthus nivalis* subsp.
>   *imperati* 'Ginns'
> *Galanthus nivalis* 'Lady Elphinstone'
> *Galanthus nivalis* 'Sandersii', see p.98

Galanthus 'Magnet'
SNOWDROP
☀ ❄❄❄ ↕ 20cm (8in) ↔ 6cm (3in)

The distinguished, scented flowers sway in the slightest breeze on their unusually long, slender stalks. This is one of the best and most reliable snowdrops. 🏆

Galanthus 'Ophelia'
SNOWDROP
☀ ❄❄❄ ↕ 15cm (6in) ↔ 20cm (8in)

A must for every collection, this very early snowdrop has fully double blooms on slender stalks. The outer segments have pinched tips, sometimes marked green.

Galanthus 'John Gray'
SNOWDROP
☀ ❄❄❄ ↕ 15cm (6in) ↔ 8cm (3in)

Exquisite and early flowering, this is one of the most collectable snowdrops. It has pendent flowers on long, slender stalks, with inner segments marked green.

Galanthus 'Mighty Atom'
SNOWDROP
☀ ❄❄❄ ↕ 12cm (5in) ↔ 8cm (3in)

An outstanding, easily grown snowdrop, bearing attractive, slender-stalked flowers with inner segments that are distinctively stained green at their tips.

Galanthus reginae-olgae
SNOWDROP
☀ ❄❄ ↕ 10cm (4in) ↔ 8cm (3in)

The earliest-flowering snowdrop, usually blooming in autumn before its green, silver-channelled leaves emerge. It is slow to increase, growing best in a sunny site.

Hellebores for Collectors

HELLEBORES ARE AMONG some of the most fashionable and collectable perennials for partially shaded sites in the garden. A wealth of named selections is rapidly becoming available, especially from China, while the range of hybrids and mixed garden seedlings already on offer is enormous.

Helleborus x *sternii* 'Boughton Beauty'
HELLEBORE
☀ ◐ ❋❋   ↕ ↔ 50cm (20in)

In late winter, green-tinted pink flowers rise above the hummock of evergreen, beautifully veined and marbled, greyish leaves. Needs protection in cold areas.

Helleborus atrorubens
HELLEBORE
☀ ❋❋❋   ↕ 30cm (12in) ↔ 45cm (18in)

A choice species, with circular, deeply divided, long-stalked leaves, often purple-tinted when young. Its starry, late winter flowers vary from deep purple to green.

Helleborus multifidus subsp. *hercegovinus*
☀ ◐ ❋❋❋   ↕ 30cm (12in) ↔ 45cm (18in)

Best known for the lacy effect of its finely dissected leaves, this hellebore also bears attractive, yellowish or pale green flowers in late winter or early spring.

Helleborus torquatus Party Dress Group
HELLEBORE
☀ ◐ ❋❋❋   ↕ 40cm (16in) ↔ 30cm (12in)

A delightful, if unusual, group of small hellebores, which produces multi-petalled flowers in a variety of colours from winter to early spring, before the leaves emerge.

Helleborus lividus
HELLEBORE
☀ ❋❋   ↕ 45cm (18in) ↔ 30cm (12in)

Silver-veined, evergreen leaves, tinted pink beneath, are accompanied by apple-green, pink-flushed flowers in winter. Best grown in an alpine house in cold areas. ♈

Helleborus odorus
HELLEBORE
☀ ◐ ❋❋❋   ↕ ↔ 50cm (20in)

This showy, easy-to-grow species is free-flowering, with masses of scented, green to yellow-green flowers in late winter or early spring. A bold, clump-forming plant.

OTHER HELLEBORES FOR COLLECTORS

Helleborus dumetorum
Helleborus x *ericsmithii*, see p.27
Helleborus x *hybridus* 'Little Black'
Helleborus x *nigercors* 'Alabaster'
Helleborus niger 'Potter's Wheel', see p.99
Helleborus purpurascens
Helleborus torquatus

Helleborus versicarius
HELLEBORE
☀ ❋❋❋   ↕ 45cm (18in) ↔ 30cm (12in)

This curious but desirable hellebore bears small, cupped, green and purple blooms in late winter and early spring, followed by inflated pods. It is dormant in summer.

Epimediums for Collectors

THE INTRODUCTION OF many new species from China has elevated epimediums to among the most collectable of perennials. As woodland plants with attractive evergreen or deciduous foliage, they form excellent ground cover, and are also effective for underplanting beneath deciduous shrubs.

Epimedium acuminatum
EPIMEDIUM

☀ ✳✳✳ ↕ 45cm (18in) ↔ 75cm (30in)

A magnificent, clump-forming evergreen with large, lance- or arrow-shaped leaflets, and long-spurred, pale purple, or purple and white flowers in spring and summer.

Epimedium davidii
EPIMEDIUM

☀ ✳✳✳ ↕ 30cm (12in) ↔ 45cm (18in)

The dark, shining stems of this choice species bear evergreen, divided leaves, and racemes of nodding, long-spurred yellow flowers from spring into summer.

OTHER EPIMEDIUMS TO COLLECT

Epimedium franchetii
Epimedium grandiflorum 'Lilafee'
Epimedium grandiflorum f. *violaceum*
Epimedium grandiflorum
  'White Queen'
Epimedium x *perralchicum* 'Wisley'
Epimedium pinnatum subsp. *colchicum*,
  see p.46
Epimedium x *versicolor* 'Sulphureum'

Epimedium grandiflorum
'Rose Queen'

☀ ✳✳✳ ↕ 30cm (12in) ↔ 45cm (18in)

The heart-shaped, prickle-toothed leaflets form a low mound and are prettily tinted when young. Showers of long-spurred, deep rose-pink flowers open in spring. 🏆

Epimedium leptorrhizum
EPIMEDIUM

☀ ✳✳✳ ↕ 25cm (10in) ↔ 45cm (18in)

In time, this creeping evergreen develops patches of stems with attractively veined, prickle-toothed leaflets. Its long-spurred flowers open in spring and early summer.

Epimedium x perralchicum
'Fröhnleiten'

☀ ✳✳✳ ↕ 40cm (16in) ↔ 60cm (24in)

Worth growing for its foliage alone, as the prickle-toothed, glossy, dark green leaves are beautifully bronze-tinted when young. Pendent spring flowers are bright yellow.

Epimedium stellulatum 'Wudang Star'
EPIMEDIUM

☀ ✳✳✳ ↕ 40cm (16in) ↔ 30cm (12in)

Multitudes of small, starry white flowers, with bold yellow beaks, are borne on wiry stems in spring above the heart-shaped, prickle-toothed, shiny, evergreen leaflets.

Epimedium x versicolor 'Versicolor'
EPIMEDIUM

☀ ✳✳✳ ↕ ↔ 30cm (12in)

This is a real charmer with its low clump of evergreen foliage, attractively tinted when young. The loose sprays of yellow, pink-suffused flowers open in spring.

Peonies for Collectors

WILD HERBACEOUS PEONIES, bearing their simple, usually single blooms of fragile petals and golden stamens, never fail to bring a touch of quality to the garden. Although their flowering period is relatively brief, they frequently have decorative foliage that extends their value in the garden.

Paeonia × smouthii
PEONY
☼ ◐ ✽✽✽✽　　　↕ ↔ 70cm (28in)

A little-known but reliable hybrid which forms clumps of finely divided leaves. It produces fragrant, cup-shaped, bright red blooms in late spring and early summer.

Paeonia cambessedesii
MAJORCAN PEONY
☼ ✽✽✽　　　↕ 55cm (22in) ↔ 60cm (24in)

Very distinctive, this peony has purple- and red-flushed stems with shiny, metallic grey-green leaves which are red or purple beneath. Spring flowers are rose-pink. ♛

Paeonia mascula subsp. *arietina*
PEONY
☼ ◐ ✽✽✽✽　　↕ 75cm (30in) ↔ 60cm (24in)

This stout clump-former has handsome, deeply divided, greyish green leaves, and bears bowl-shaped, reddish pink flowers with creamy yellow stamens during spring.

> **OTHER PEONIES TO COLLECT**
>
> *Paeonia clusii*
> *Paeonia obovata*
> *Paeonia obovata* var. *alba*
> *Paeonia peregrina* 'Otto Froebel'
> *Paeonia tenuifolia* 'Rosea'
> *Paeonia veitchii* var. *woodwardii*
> *Paeonia* 'White Wings'
> *Paeonia* 'Whitleyi Major'
> *Paeonia wittmanniana* 'Yao-huang'

Paeonia tenuifolia
PEONY
☼ ✽✽✽　　　　　　↕ ↔ 45cm (18in)

Quite unlike any other species, this forms bold clumps of beautiful, finely dissected leaves. The cupped, deep red flowers are borne in late spring and early summer.

Paeonia emodi
HIMALAYAN PEONY
☼ ◐ ✽✽✽　　　　　↕ ↔ 80cm (32in)

In late spring, slightly nodding, cupped, fragrant white flowers are carried by the handsome clump of branched stems with deeply divided leaves. Enjoys a shady site.

Paeonia mlokosewitschii
CAUCASIAN PEONY
☼ ◐ ✽✽✽✽　　　　↕ ↔ 70cm (28in)

This well-known peony has stout clumps of downy, grey-green leaves. Its lemon-yellow, late-spring and summer blooms are followed by brilliant red seed capsules.

Paeonia wittmanniana
PEONY
☼ ◐ ✽✽✽✽　　　　↕ ↔ 90cm (36in)

An outstanding species, with bold clumps of glossy, dark green leaves. Bowl-shaped, pale yellow flowers, borne from late spring to summer, are followed by red seed pods.

SPECIALIST PLANTS

INDEX

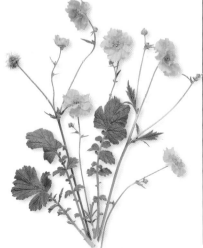

T

Acknowledgments

AUTHOR'S ACKNOWLEDGMENTS
Once again, I am indebted to my wife Sue who somehow made time in a busy life to decipher and type my handwritten notes for this book. My thanks also to Hatton Gardner for checking the index, and to David Barker, Joyce Cama, Cliff Dad, Dilys Davies, Pat Jackson, Danae Johnston,

Chris Mortimer, Bob Mousley, and Ray Wilson of the Hardy Plant Society, who kindly helped with suggestions, as did Sarah Drew, Jean Fletcher, Hala Humphries, Sabine Liebherr, and George Smith. Beyond these few are the many who have encouraged my interest in perennials over the years. To all of you, my heartfelt thanks. Last but certainly not least, my editorial team, initially Lesley Malkin and Colin Walton, but principally Anna Cheifetz and Helen Robson, who must have sweated at times over my schedule but remained calm and focused throughout. Thanks for your patience, guidance, and gentle prodding.

DORLING KINDERSLEY would like to thank Howard Rice for all his additional help, Ann Kay for proof reading, Lesley Malkin and Colin Walton for their support and initial work on this project, and Simon Maughan for image scanning.

PHOTOGRAPHY CREDITS
Key: l=left, r=right, t=top, c=centre, b=bottom
Commissioned photographs: Howard Rice, Colin Walton, and Andrew Henley; **additional pictures:** Clive Boursnell, Deni Bown, Jonathan Buckley, Andrew Butler, Eric Crichton, Andrew de Lory, Christine Douglas, John Fielding, Neil Fletcher, John Glover, Derek Hall, Jerry Harpur, Sunniva Harte, Neil Holmes, Andrew Lawson, Howard Rice, Robert Rundle, Juliette Wade, Colin Walton, Matthew Ward, and Steven Wooster.
Agency photographs: Garden Picture Library: John Glover 2, 12br, 88tr, 136bl; Steven Wooster 14br, 42bl, 113; **Jerry Harpur** (designer: Sheila

McQueen): 9b; **Andrew Lawson** (designer: Wendy Lauderdale): 14bl; **Scope Features:** Steve Poole 8tr; **Derek St Romaine:** 11tr; **Howard Rice:** 4, 9tr, 10bl, 10br, 11tl, 13tl, 13tr, 13br, 15, 27bm, 27tr, 39br, 42br, 43, 70tl, 70bl, 70bm, 70br, 71bm, 71tr, 88bl, 88br, 89, 97bm, 112bl, 112tr, 134bl, 137; **Roy Lancaster:** 8bl, 22tl, 22bl, 24bl, 30bl, 30tc, 31tr, 36tr, 38tr, 40br, 64tl, 76tr, 83bm, 98bl, 102tm, 11bm, 118tr, 123tm, 123bm, 127tr, 128mr, 133mm, 134bl, 134bm, 135tr, 136tr, 139br, 142bm, 143tl, 147br, 148ml, 148tm, 148mr; **Matthew Ward:** 10tl, 12ml (containers by Malcolm Hillier).

PHOTOGRAPHERS' ACKNOWLEDGMENTS
In England: Alan Shipp, Beth Chatto Gardens, Bressingham Gardens, Broadlands Gardens, Cambridge Alpines, Cambridge Bulbs, Cambridge Garden Plants, Cambridge University Botanic Gardens, David Austin Roses Ltd., Fulbrooke Nursery, Goldbrooke Plants, Hadlow College, Hopleys Plants Ltd., John Morley, Langthorns Plantery, Monksilver Nursery, Paradise Centre, Peter Lewis, Potterton and Martin, Rickard's Hardy Ferns, Mrs. Sally Edwards, West Acre Gardens. **In Australia:** Birchfield Herbs (Marcia Voce), Buskers End (Joan Arnold), Elizabeth Town Nursery (John and Corrie Dudley), Essie Huxley, Garden of St. Erth, Island Bulbs (Kevin Fagan, Viv Hale), Lambley Nursery (David Glenn), Moidart Wholesale Nursery (Graham Warwick), Otto Fauser, Penny Dunn, Rosevears Nursery (Rachael Howell) Sally Johansohn, Suz Price, Theresa Watts, Woodbank Nursery (Ken Gallander), Yates.